The
CINEMA
of
BASEBALL

Baseball and American Society
Series ISBN 0-88736-566-3

1. Blackball Stars
John B. Holway
ISBN 0-88736-094-7   CIP 1988

2. Baseball History, Premier Edition
Edited by Peter Levine
ISBN 0-88736-288-5   1988

3. My 9 Innings: An Autobiography of 50 Years in Baseball
Lee MacPhail
ISBN 0-88736-387-3   CIP 1989

4. Black Diamonds: Life in the Negro Leagues from the Men Who Lived It
John B. Holway
ISBN 0-88736-334-2   CIP 1989

5. Baseball History 2
Edited by Peter Levine
ISBN 0-88736-342-3   1989

6. Josh and Satch: A Dual Biography of Josh Gibson and Satchel Paige
John B. Holway
ISBN 0-88736-333-4   CIP 1991

7. Encyclopedia of Major League Baseball Team Histories
Edited by Peter C. Bjarkman
Volume 1: American League
ISBN 0-88736-373-3   CIP 1991

8. Encyclopedia of Major League Baseball Team Histories
Edited by Peter C. Bjarkman
Volume 2: National League
ISBN 0-88736-374-1   CIP 1991

9. Baseball History 3
Edited by Peter Levine
ISBN 0-88736-577-9   1990

10. The Immortal Diamond: Baseball in American Literature
Peter C. Bjarkman
ISBN 0-88736-481-0 (hardcover)   CIP forthcoming, 1991
ISBN 0-88736-482-9 (softcover)   CIP forthcoming, 1991

11. Total Latin American Baseball
Peter C. Bjarkman
ISBN 0-88736-546-9   CIP forthcoming, 1992

12. Baseball Players and Their Times: A History of the Major Leagues, 1920–1940
Eugene Murdock
ISBN 0-88736-235-4   CIP 1991

13. The Tropic of Baseball: Baseball in the Dominican Republic
Rob Ruck
ISBN 0-88736-707-0   CIP 1991

14. The Cinema of Baseball: Images of America, 1929–1989
Gary E. Dickerson
ISBN 0-88736-710-0   CIP 1991

15. Baseball History 4
Edited by Peter Levine
ISBN 0-88736-578-7   CIP forthcoming, 1991

16. Baseball and American Society: A Textbook of Baseball History
Peter C. Bjarkman
ISBN 0-88736-483-7 (softcover)   CIP forthcoming, 1992

17. Cooperstown Symposium on
Baseball and the American Culture (1989)
Edited by Alvin L. Hall
ISBN 0-88736-719-4   CIP 1991

18. Cooperstown Symposium on
Baseball and the American Culture (1990)
Edited by Alvin L. Hall
ISBN 0-88736-735-6   CIP forthcoming

The
CINEMA
of
BASEBALL:

▲ ▲ ▲

IMAGES OF AMERICA, 1929-1989

Gary E. Dickerson

Meckler
Westport ▪ London

Library of Congress Cataloging-in-Publication Data

Dickerson, Gary E.
  The cinema of baseball : images of America, 1929-1989 / Gary E.
Dickerson.
    p. cm. -- (Baseball and American society ; 14)
    Includes bibliographical references (p.   ) and index.
    ISBN 0-88736-710-0 : $
    1. Baseball films. 2. Motion pictures--Social aspects--United
States. 3. United States in motion pictures.   I. Title.
II. Series.
PN1995.9.B28D5   1991
791.43'655--dc20   91-8510
                                              CIP

British Library Cataloguing-in-Publication Data is available.

Meckler Publishing, the publishing division of Meckler Corporation,
  11 Ferry Lane West, Westport, CT 06880.
Meckler Ltd., 247-249 Vauxhall Bridge Road,
  London SW1V 1HQ, U.K.

Printed on acid free paper.
Printed and bound in the United States of America.

Contents

Acknowledgments

Most of the material contained in this book was originally included in my Ph.D. dissertation, completed in August 1989 at Bowling Green State University. While there were many scholars who made contributions to the original piece, one clearly stands out from among the rest. It is with a deep sense of gratitude that I thank Dr. Jack Nachbar for the encouragement, direction, and criticism he gave throughout this project. I am also grateful to Heidelberg College personnel for their support and the use of Heidelberg's facilities. Nancy Brodman and Mary Puffenberger deserve special mention and thanks for the preparation of the various drafts of this manuscript. Many thanks are extended to Lee Strickland, the film library at the University of Wisconsin, Madison, and the Motion Picture Broadcasting and Recorded Sound Division of the Library of Congress in Washington, D.C., all of which assisted me in procuring copies of several of the older baseball films viewed for this project.

Of course, this work would not have begun and certainly would not have been completed had it not been for the loving support and encouragement I received from my best friend and wife, Janet; my sons: Joshua, Micah, Joel and Benjamin; and Joe and Lucy Feldmann. Loving appreciation and respect must also be given to my parents and my creator for providing me with the necessary "tools" to accomplish all that I have. Finally, tribute must be paid to the filmic Roy Hobbs and to the "Shoeless One," Joe Jackson for being "the best there ever was."

Gary E. Dickerson

Introduction

A t some point in the history of American sports, immediately following the Civil War (see Lucas and Smith's *Saga of American Sport* 1978, 170 and Guttman's *From Ritual to Record* 1978, 95), the game of baseball became known as "America's favorite pastime." A passage from a Minnesota newspaper in 1867 reported:

> The game of baseball has become so much the style that nearly every village and hamlet has its club, and to be a member of the first nine is now looked upon as being nearly as honorable a position as a seat in the legislature (Monroe 1938, 181).

Authors John Lucas and Ronald Smith state that no other sport from the Civil War to World War I

> dominated the sport scene for the American masses as did baseball . . . the masses took it as their game, a symbol of exuberant, individualistic, and driving spirit (Lucas and Smith 1978, 170).

Mark Twain called baseball the symbol of America and said it was "the outward and visible expression, of the drive and push and rush and struggle of the raging, tearing, and booming of the nineteenth century" (Clemens 1923, 145). At the turn of the nineteenth century, Americans were increasingly becoming more sport-conscious and as such embraced baseball as "their" game.

Some scholars have indicated that America's interest in sports in the late nineteenth and early twentieth centuries is significant because of the role that sports played as a democratizing agent. Immigrants, during this time period, shared in the sporting experience and spirit that was becoming a symbol of the American tradition.

> At sporting contests, first or second generation Americans could identify with many of the traditional American values so greatly mirrored in American sport. The drive of hope for the future, the

1

demand for leadership and cooperation, the worship of the individual hero, and the outpouring of the national spirit. . . . All
could be found in the ritualized organized sport of the late nineteenth and early twentieth centuries. Sport more than some areas
of society, may have served as a democratizing agent for the
masses of immigrants who came to America from the 1850s to
the time of World War I (Lucas and Smith 1978, 145).

Robert Peterson asserts in *Only the Ball Was White* (1970) that the
baseball field is the only place in the world where social barriers are broken
down and that economic status and breeding are not as important as who
plays the best baseball (Peterson 1970, 31). Scholars seem to agree that baseball reflects American culture and the values associated with that culture.
Baseball is a game for *all* Americans.

Several scholars in the area of film studies have attributed similar
democratizing characteristics to the film medium. For example, Garth Jowett
contends in *Film: The Democratic Art* (1976):

For the immigrant worker, the movies provided more than just a
way of filling-in time, but also acted as a guide to the newcomer
on the manners and customs of his new environment (Jowett
1976, 36).

In Movie-Made America (1976) Robert Sklar argues that,

The movies were not simply gathering places where. . . sins were
committed; they were centers of communication and cultural dif-
fusion (Sklar 1976, 18).

Other film scholars have maintained that the movies act as a mirror
of the culture that produces them. Andrew Bergman points out in *We're in
the Money* (1971):

As films are not viewed in a void, neither are they created in a
void. Every movie is a cultural artifact . . . and as such reflects
the fears, values, myths, and assumptions of the culture that produces it (Bergman 1971, XII).

Sam Grogg and Jack Nachbar, in the introduction to *Movies as Artifacts: Cultural Criticism of Popular Film* (1982) assert that "American movies have always been commercial products made to appeal to the desires and
tastes of a mass audience" (Marsden, Nachbar, and Grogg, eds. 1982, 8).

Finally, Siegfried Kracauer, in his seminal 1947 work *From Caligari to Hitler*, states that "The films of a nation reflect its mentality in a more direct way than other artistic media" (Kracauer 1947, 5).

What was being communicated and diffused via the silent screen to the immigrants, were some of the same images and values of contemporary America that were being communicated through baseball, i.e., the American competitive spirit and sense of fair play, the virtue of hard work, the virtue of recreation and the promise of success. It would appear then that these two entertainment media, baseball and the movies, share some rather noteworthy characteristics. Specifically, scholars from a variety of disciplines have asserted that both baseball and the cinema have assisted in enculturating the American people and are, in fact, instructional tools by which Americans have learned and acquired American values and culture.

If the premise that baseball is or was "America's Game" is accurate and as such, it can be said to reflect the popular values of American culture, and if the premise that film reflects the popular values of American culture is accurate, then it seems logical that a study that has the exploration of the values contained in baseball films as its focus would be valuable as a tool for discovering what these values are and what they suggest about our culture. Therefore, two of the most important questions this book will attempt to answer is, "What are the popular American values reflected in feature length baseball films from 1929 to 1989 and what do these values tell us about American culture during this time period?"

One of the goals of this study is to isolate changes that occur in the dominant values depicted in these baseball films. By comparing and contrasting the values in each film period, explanations and insights that lead to understanding these changes should become apparent.

The impetus for this study is provided in part by the need to verify that both film and baseball enculturate the masses and reflect popular values. Impetus is also provided by the need to explain why filmmakers have repeatedly chosen to make films about baseball even when baseball films have generally resulted in only mediocre financial success. For example, of the forty-one commercial sound films that are included in this study, less than twenty-five percent have had relative success at the box office. On the other hand, ten films produced after 1950, which is almost one-half of all those produced during this period, grossed under one million dollars.

There are additional data that enhance the curious status of baseball films. The production of baseball films has been noticeably more prolific in some eras than in others, and there have been extended periods that produced no baseball films at all. For example, there were seventeen baseball films released from 1948 to 1958 (at least one in each of those years except 1955). However, only two baseball films were released from 1959 to 1976. What was special about the 1950s that would produce a seemingly receptive climate for the stories told or values conveyed in baseball films? How does each baseball film era relate to the climate or attitude of the viewing audience or popular American values in each era? Providing answers to these questions is another goal of this book.

The level and intensity of sports interest in the U.S. continues to grow and has gone well beyond being merely a spectator's concern, a pastime, or just another mode of entertainment in an entertainment-obsessed culture. Professional and amateur sports are politically, economically, socially, and legally intertwined with our nation's infrastructure. City planners routinely consider the potential of attracting major league sports teams when planning the addition of a large multipurpose convention hall or arena. American sports are considered serious business. American sports communicate notions to us about ourselves and our values. Our history and our national image are casually associated with "being a good sport."

Still most of us have yet to regard the serious study of what sport communicates to us as being truly worthwhile. Communication researchers, scholars, and academicians have just begun to regard sports communication as a legitimate area of scholastic endeavor. Allen Guttman points out that Max Scheler, writing in 1927, noted that even though sport had "grown immeasurably in scope and importance, the meaning of sport had received little in the way of serious attention." Guttman further observes that "Sports remain among the most discussed and least understood phenomena of our time" (Guttman 1977, I).

This condition has not changed significantly in the last ten years. The more contemporary works that have been published on sports, e.g., *Cosell* (1973), *SuperTube: The Rise of Television Sports* (1984), and *Voices of the Game* (1987), have come from sports insiders and not communication scholars. The majority of contemporary academicians still regard sports as frivolity. It seems reasonable to conclude, however, that there needs to be more serious research done in the area of sports communication. More research could help answer questions like, "Why are sports so important to us as a nation?"

Yet another dimension of this study's significance is in the area of sociocultural film analysis. A sociocultural analysis assumes that a film or any cultural artifact is not created in a vacuum. Rather it reflects, in a variety of ways, the culture that produced the artifact. Therefore, an intense examination of a cultural artifact will produce meaningful conclusions about the values of the culture producing the artifact. Kathy Merlock Jackson writes in *Images of Children in American Film* (1986) that:

For the sociocultural film scholar, films, and the images generated in them, are representative of the underlying beliefs of the people who make and view them (Jackson 1986, 4).

Beginning with Siegfried Kracauer's *From Caligari to Hitler* (1947), the movement to regard a nation's films as a unit of historical and sociocultural analysis has grown stronger. However, there are still relatively few major works that utilize the sociocultural perspective. Ideally, each successive work employing this approach adds to our understanding of our culture, values, history and attitudes toward a variety of subjects, e.g., women, blacks, children, and the Depression. Hopefully, the work presented here, with its focus on baseball, adds to the body of works that employ sociocultural film analysis and hence adds to our understanding of our attitudes and values about our nation's sports heroes and related issues.

Finally, there is significance in this study as it relates to the film genre. The sports film seems to have been overlooked as a major film genre. I believe the sports film is a special kind of film with special conventions and narrative patterns that is potentially meaningful as a genre study. It is hoped that this study will at least lay the ground work and act as an impetus for further study in the area of film genres.

Defining a Baseball Film

The baseball films included in this study were produced and released in the "sound" years from 1929 through 1989. Only feature-length commercial films are included in this investigation. This limitation is imposed upon the study as an attempt to standardize the artifact as much as possible. By eliminating documentaries, newsreels, cartoons, and silent films, comparisons and conclusions made regarding the images and values expressed in the various films become more reliable, valid, and accurate.

In addition, the films included in this study are *primarily* about baseball. In other words, a film in which a game of baseball is played once or twice, or in which a principal character was once a baseball player but beyond that there is little reference to baseball, or a film in which baseball is casually mentioned, or a film that is about softball rather than baseball, is not considered a baseball film. Examples of films where baseball is an insignificant part of the film and therefore not addressed here include: *Brother Rat* (1938), *About Face* (1952), *The Chosen* (1982), *Max Dugan Returns* (1983), and *Stealing Home* (1988). In *The Chosen,* two Jewish boys become friends after meeting in a softball game. Although there may be significance in the fact that their friendship originates around baseball-like conditions, there is no reference to baseball. The film is primarily about being Jewish in America. *Brother Rat* and *About Face*, a musical remake of *Brother Rat*, are more about being in military school than they are about baseball. Although the three main characters in each of these two films are on the school's baseball team and even though there might be some interesting associations made in the films between military rules and baseball rules, the films use baseball only as a subtext to develop themes that focus primarily upon military academies, their rules and regulations, military relationships, and the predicaments that these young men get themselves into by not following military rules. In *Max Dugan Returns*, Max Dugan hires a big league batting coach to help his grandson hit a home run on the high school baseball team. However, the film is really about Max Dugan returning to the family he deserted long ago and whether or not he stole the money he lavishly spends on his reclaimed family. Similarly, *Stealing Home* seems to be a story of a man coming to grips with his own life and identity after a close friend commits suicide. The protagonist plays high school baseball at the beginning of the film and joins a semi-pro team at the conclusion of the film, but most of everything in between has little to do with baseball.

One film that presents somewhat of a problem, given the above definition, is *The Bad News Bears Go to Japan* (1978). The film actually has very little to do with baseball. In fact, there are only three scenes where a baseball game, of sorts, is actually played. However, the film is categorized as a baseball film because of the history that accompanies the Bears players from the first film of the Bad News Bears trilogy, *The Bad News Bears* (1976), in which they appeared.

For this study, films will be regarded as baseball films if the following criteria are met: (1) The principal character (or characters) plays, coaches, or has more than a casual association with the game of baseball, and (2) the narrative must, either explicitly or implicitly, be principally about baseball. There seems to be no way to further define a baseball film. If an attempt were made to establish an approximate amount of time that a film must devote to baseball in order to be defined as a baseball film, the end result would be no clearer. Using time to measure the content of a film's narrative becomes awkward when attempting to differentiate between film time and real time.

Forty-one films fall within the operational definition established above for baseball films. Out of these forty-one films, I have viewed thirty-one either on film or video tape and, in some cases, both. Most of the viewing of these films occurred between September and December of 1988. The non-viewed films were not available on video tape or film at the Library of Congress in Washington, D.C., the University of Wisconsin—Madison or from a variety of video tape sources (see the Appendix for a complete baseball film listing). Film reviews and articles were consulted as secondary sources especially in cases where viewing the film was not possible.

The films addressed in this book are not limited to films that were box-office hits. Less successful baseball films add information or reinforce information about popular values and attitudes that would be missed by looking only at the "hits." As Kracauer maintains in *From Caligari to Hitler*,

> What counts is not so much the statistically measureable popularity of films as the popularity of their pictorial and narrative motifs. Persistent reiterations of these motifs marks them as outward projections of inner urges (Kracauer 1947, 8).

However, when a particular film's popularity is exceptional, when compared to others of the same era or kind, attempts are made to account for the popularity.

Identifying the recurring and dominant values portrayed in the baseball films of each era requires that each era have a point of demarkation. In this study, the eras are noted not necessarily by decades and years but rather by the closeness in proximity of a group of films released. For example, the films released from 1929 to 1935 constitute one era because only the year 1931 did not produce a baseball film. The next era covers only 1942 and 1943, since there was a six-year absence of baseball films prior to 1942 and a four-year absence of baseball films following 1943.

The dominant values in these films are identified by examining the character traits attributed to the films' protagonists. The primary baseball character(s) in the films, or the protagonist, is developed in each film and is given, by his or her creator, specific characteristics or traits. I am using the term *creator* to connote all those creatively involved with the production of the films. These traits include elements such as moral standards, birthplace, hometown, upbringing, desires, and demeanor. Of interest in this study is the presence and recurrence of these traits. The inference here is that these traits represent the composite traits of the Hollywood-created baseball player. This mythical or filmic baseball player would possess the stereotypic traits, values, and images that the creators think the film audience has of real baseball heroes. My assumption is that the Hollywood version of the baseball player is the embodiment of the popular ideals and values held by the audience members at the time the film was released. The dominant and recurring traits given to the protagonist in each film era will serve as symbols of the values of that era, and they will be analyzed and explained within the sociocultural context of that era.

The Observation Process

In order to establish which values are present in each film era in a more me-thodical and rigorous fashion, I have chosen to use a paradigm derived from Robert Ray's *A Certain Tendency of the Hollywood Cinema, 1930-1980* (1985), as a gauge for measuring these values. Ray asserts that classical Hollywood cinema has traditionally relied upon the development of characters who are basically two-sided. Ray also claims that:

> Such two-sided characters seemed particularly designed to appeal to a collective American imagination steeped in myths of inclu-siveness . . . The movies traded on one opposition in particular, American culture's traditional dichotomy of individual and com-munity that had generated the most significant pair of competing myths: the outlaw hero and the official hero (Ray 1985, 58-59).

Ray emphasizes that such a significant amount of Hollywood mate-rial plays upon this natural/outlaw hero versus the civilized/official hero di-chotomy that it has become "the main tendency of American literature" and by logical extension Hollywood (Ray 1985, 59). Ray indicates that three sets of competing values surface from this natural versus civilized dichotomy (at times in this work, I have chosen to substitute the terms *natural* and *civilized* respectively, for Ray's *outlaw* and *official*): youth and aging; society and women; and politics and the law. A brief description of the three sets of com-peting values is offered below.

Regarding the value of *aging*, Ray asserts that the natural hero or what he calls the "outlaw hero" is more inclined to display behavior that is childlike, whimsical, flighty, and emotionally based. The natural hero is gen-erally somewhat immature as opposed to the civilized hero who is more adult-like, reasonable, logical, wise, pensive, and rational.

Characterizing the value of *society and women*, Ray maintains that the natural hero tends to see the institution of marriage as a representation of the society that he is either not a part of or that he typically distrusts. Society tends to place restrictions, norms, and boundaries around the natural hero's personality, and these boundaries confine the number of choices he can make. Ideally, the natural hero rejects or ignores society's restrictions. Women, as the embodiment of society, typically represent obstacles or the entanglements of society for the natural hero. The natural hero's view of women generally leads to anxiety and internal or external conflict because on one hand, he is biologically attracted to them, but on the other hand, he cannot psychological-ly resolve the conflict that arises from what they represent, namely, formal society and responsibility.

Conversely, the civilized hero is typically at ease with women. The responsibilities of community and public service do not necessarily represent confinement to him. In fact, the civilized hero views public service to his community as a welcomed obligation. He is concerned about the welfare of his community, and the wife or woman in his life typically symbolizes the strength that he needs to carry out his public duties. He subscribes to the notion that the family, societal norms, and proper codes of conduct are necessary for a strong community.

Finally, Ray posits that *politics and law* represent the third set of contrasting values. Since both of these institutions are manifestations of a larger society, the natural hero is inclined to view them as ineffective and impersonal. The individualism that typically characterizes the natural hero is disavowed in a politicized society where laws are constructed for the good of the greater community. The natural hero is much more inclined to live by an internalized code of good and bad and right and wrong, whereas the civilized hero is inclined to adhere to the philosophies that "No man can put himself above the law" and "You can not take the law into your own hands." The natural hero is likely to be a proponent of credos like "Grab the bull by the horns" and "If you want to get anything done, do it yourself." In contrast, the civilized hero is more apt to believe in the ability of "the system" to work and he is more likely to abide by the rules and codes of the "Greater Society."

By employing the paradigm outlined above, it is presumed that the characterizations of the protagonists, in the films under investigation here, are developed along the lines of the natural hero or the civilized hero. But as Ray suggests, it is also likely that in some instances both sets of values will exist concurrently in the same era, the same film, or in the same hero. This does not seem to be problematic. In fact, it seems more realistic to view the two sets of conflicting values on a continuum. In other words, it is quite possible that one hero possesses natural, as well as, civilized hero tendencies.

Explanation and understanding of each era's position on the natural hero/civilized hero continuum becomes meaningful when the film era is viewed within its proper sociocultural context. To summarize, it is the intent of this study to look for the presence, recurrence, and repetitive use of the aforementioned sets of values in baseball films from 1929 to 1989 and relate those findings to the cultural context.

It is important to note, at this point, that the audience can perceive both the natural hero and the civilized hero traditions as containing positive and negative values. In Ray's discussion of the outlaw hero and official hero, he maintains that:

If the extreme individualism of the outlaw hero always verged on selfishness, the respectability of the official hero always threatened to involve either blandness or repression. If the outlaw tradition promised adventure and freedom, it also offered danger and loneliness. If the official tradition promised safety and comfort, it also offered entanglements and boredom (Ray 1985, 62-63).

Hence each tradition plays a dynamic role with regard to what the audiences find attractive, and each tradition is typically portrayed not in an absolute form but used in some combination of the opposite tradition.

The implication here is not that each and every audience member processes the same meaning from the character traits portrayed in the film nor that the significance of the trait is the same for every viewer. Certainly some viewers may not even be aware of the implicit or explicit values given the protagonist by the film's creators, since each viewer has his/her own symbol processing system and each system is somewhat different from any other. Yet, filmmakers rely on the fact that film audiences share certain common experiences, values, and thoughts. By appropriately depicting those experiences, thoughts, and values in their films, the creators achieve the desired response from the audience. These shared experiences supply the basis for mass popularity and mass communication. Tony Schwartz, in his book *The Responsive Chord* (1973), alludes to this concept:

> To achieve a behavioral effect whether persuading someone to buy a product or teaching a person about history, one designs stimuli that will resonate with the elements in a communication environment to produce that effect (Schwartz 1973, 26).

What is implied here is that the values depicted in these baseball films are representative of the values of the movie audiences which are, in turn, representative of the values of the greater population, independent of baseball or sports. In other words, the values depicted in the baseball films are taken to be representative of society's values of the idealized American hero in the particular era in which the films were released.

It is clear to this researcher that the baseball films included in this study were not created exclusively to transmit or reflect cultural values. Obviously each film has entertainment value for the viewing public and therefore potential profit value for the creator. However, it seems unlikely that the viewer would be entertained by a film and attracted to a film that did not at least reinforce values already embraced, whether or not the viewer was cognizant of that fact. Andrew Bergman's statement "People do not escape into something they cannot relate to" (Bergman 1971, XII) is useful here. The logical extension of this statement is that audiences are not entertained by something they cannot relate to. John O'Connor and Martin Jackson assert that:

The value of entertainment films will become more evident if we consider them as we do popular novels, as cultural documents, rather than comparing them with traditional records and archival manuscripts. It is precisely because such films are made for entertainment that they have value for the historian. They tell us what made people of other decades laugh or cry, what made them forget their troubles, and what they believed about their past. The popular movie stereotypes of women, Indians, blacks, and other ethnic and cultural groups, may tell the historian more than any other source can about the subtleties of mass prejudice. And changing tastes in movie fare from decade to decade and year to year may help us to understand the changing values and concerns of people over time (O'Connor and Jackson 1979, XVII).

Explanation of Sociocultural Analysis

A sociocultural analysis, such as the one being conducted here, places the film into the context of its culture so that economic, political, historical, and other social and cultural factors are taken into account. These factors are considered when the sociocultural scholar attempts to explain the presence of a particular theme, motif, image or value in a particular film. The sociocultural scholar assumes that *everything* that appears in a film is there for a reason. Images and traits do not appear in a commercial feature film by accident. The sociocultural film scholar attempts to account for the continued presence of a particular theme, value, motif, or trait and/or the change or absence of those particular elements throughout a body of films or a single film.

Several scholars, e.g., Kracauer, Sklar, Jowett, and Bergman, have effectively used the sociocultural methodology for exploring popular values and images reflected in film. According to Allen and Gomery, "The seminal historical account of the relationship between film and society" is Kracauer's *From Caligari to Hitler* (Allen and Gomery 1985, 159). Kracauer looked at approximately one hundred films of pre-Nazi Germany in search of the national mentality that was ripe for Hitler. However, Allen and Gomery appropriately point out that Kracauer's methodological shortcomings left his work open to some important criticisms.

Kracauer's vague criteria for determining which films contained these pictorial and narrative motifs and what constituted persistent reiteration of them combined with his unsubstantiated claim that these motifs pervaded films of all levels, and left his work open to methodological question, particularly by empiricists, historians, and sociologists (Allen and Gomery 1985, 164).

Probably the most complete sociocultural film analyses to date are

Robert Sklar's *Movie-Made America* (1976) and Garth Jowett's *Film: The Democratic Art* (1976). The focus of these two works is the social history of the development of American films, who made them and why. The scope of these works is much broader than the present study and both are much more concerned with the development of the film industry than is this study.

Andrew Bergman's *We're in the Money* is a sociocultural film analysis that attempts to account for the value and popularity of over eighty Depression era films in the United States. Bergman attempts to find out why film-going was such an important event for a nation whose people were so down and out. Bergman concludes his Depression era film study by saying:

> The movies made a central contribution toward educating Americans in the fact that wrongs could be set right within their existing institutions. . . . They showed that individual initiative still bred success, that the federal government was a benevolent watchman, that we were a classless, melting pot nation (Bergman 1971, 167-168).

More recent sociocultural film studies include: Kathy Merlock-Jackson's *Images of Children in American Film* (1986), Kenneth MacKinnon's *Hollywood's Small Towns* (1984), and Les and Barbara Keyser's *Hollywood and the Catholic Church* (1984). All these works examine various aspects of American society using various films as guides to the popular images and values held by the American masses. These studies have added not only to our knowledge about our culture but also to the utility and popularity of the sociocultural methodology.

Yet, the precise methodological technique utilized in these works is not always clear. It is obvious that the authors viewed several films and read several articles and texts relevant to their topics. However, the specifics on how they arrived at their conclusions based on an application of a sociocultural model is unclear to the reader. This kind of eclectic approach tends to give empiricist scholars some real difficulty. Too much seems to be left to the critic's discretion. It is incumbent upon this researcher to design a more clearly structured model for analyzing films.

No film study to date, sociocultural or otherwise, has focused upon the sports film in a scholarly and analytical fashion. This study is the first.

Baseball Films in the Depression Era

T he thirteen years that preceded the release of Warner Bros.' *Fireman, Save My Child* (1932), the first film I viewed for this study, was a time of intense and rapid change in the United States. The turn of events that occurred in these years caused major attitude shifts in America. Many had hoped that the end of the war would immediately bring new prosperity and a world safe for democracy. However, following the war, older Americans seemed fed up with idealistic causes that they had championed during the Wilson presidency while young Americans were typically cynical and disenchanted with the world that they had inherited from their elders (Morris 1947, 68-69). The American mood changed to confidence and optimism on the heels of the prosperous twenties. But the confidence and optimism of the twenties quickly turned to almost complete despair following the stock market crash in 1929 (Allen 1931, 394).

Several events that occured in the twenties are significant for establishing a context for the initial baseball film period. According to Dale Somers, the year 1920 was significant because it marked the end of a leisure revolution in the United States.

> Throughout the colonial period and the early years of the republic, Americans adhered fairly rigidly to the gospel of work, which stressed the value of labor and frowned upon the pursuit of pleasure . . . Pleasure-seeking certainly occupied a low position in the typical American's scale of values before 1820 . . . Enthusiasm for recreation on a great scale developed rapidly as the United States shifted from rural-agrarian to an urban-industrial society (Somers 1971, 125-6).

Lucas and Smith state that the situation in the United States at the turn of the century and into the twenties was ripe for a sporting explosion due in part to the decline of religious opposition to recreation, an increase in the

13

number of immigrants arriving in America and their subsequent emigration to the cities, growing prosperity, and the sporting atmosphere promoted by President Theodore Roosevelt.

Of all the factors impacting upon the sporting and recreation revolution, none seems more important than the new wealth and abundant leisure time provided the average American by the industrial-urban growth (Lucas and Smith 1978, 145). For the average urban American, the continued technological and industrial growth occurring in the United States at this time meant larger paychecks and shorter working hours. This translated into more leisure time and more expendable income than most Americans had ever known. Historian George Mowry states: "For the first time in world history the masses of a great nation had not only bread but cake" (Mowry 1963, 3).

In addition, Mowry claims that the twenties represent the formative years of modern industrialized America.

> The period was one of amazing vitality, of social invention and change. . . . It was during these years that the country first became urban, particularly in the cast of its mind, in its ideals, and in its folk ways. Interwoven and interacting with this change was an amazing technological development and the rise of a new type of industrial economy typified by mass production and mass consumption. Both factors speeded the breakdown of old habits and patterns of thought and prepared the way for the future (Mowry 1963, 1).

Undoubtedly, one of the old habits and patterns of thought that Mowry refers to here is morality. Morality changed dramatically in the twenties. Garth Jowett notes that it was this revolution in morals "which created the bitter conflicts between the representatives of traditional culture and those who favored the new order" (Jowett 1976, 141).

Alcohol consumption was one of the major suspects blamed for the alleged decline in morality. When the proponents of prohibition finally won their battle in January of 1919, it appeared that public officials had made some headway in curtailing the country's declining moral trends. In actuality, prohibition was to have little positive impact upon the traditional American moral standards. If anything, the inability to enforce prohibition under the Volstead Act and the increase in female drinkers after the legislation was enacted further contributed to the weakening of morals in America (Mowry 1965, 26).

The movies during this "Jazz Age" became a primary target of moral reformers. Reformers believed that the movies, more than any other factor, were responsible for the moral revolution. This belief was based on the fact that so many people, especially the young, frequented the movies. "The movies became, without doubt, the most popular entertainment of the "Jazz Age" (Jowett 1976, 186).

By 1922, the pressure upon the film industry to clean up its act was becoming so great and was coming from so many different sources that the film industry felt compelled to appoint Will Hays, the Postmaster General during the Harding Administration, to preside over a newly formed industry organization (Sklar 1976, 83). The creation of this organization, eventually called the Motion Picture Producers and Distributors of America (MPPDA), was intended to quell the widespread criticism and dissatisfaction expressed by the leading reformers. To this end, Hays achieved only limited success. Hays headed up the MPPDA until 1945 (Jowett 1976, 181).

In addition, reformers made attempts to control fashion and the "new" dances, dances where men and women embraced and danced cheek-to-cheek, dances that were condemned by religious leaders and elected officials. These and other attempts to turn the tide of moral degradation proved ineffective. Corruption and vice remained commonplace throughout the United States during the twenties.

A new intellectual revolution that came into vogue after the conclusion of the war also received some of the blame for the nation's morality swoon. Historian Lloyd Morris attributes the moral decline during the twenties to this new revolution.

> An intellectual revolution took place between the end of the Great War and the onset of the Great Depression. When it had run its course, many things were changed. Manners and morals were different. The American cultural heritage was in disrepute. The authority of the past had been broken. The example of precedent was heavily discounted. A structure of values slowly built and long established had swiftly collapsed. Familiar ideals had the look of old illusions that are dead forever. The new generation was thinking about American life in a new way (Morris 1947, 148-149).

Permissive sexual behavior that was made fashionable by the introduction of Freudian psychology became very popular with the young and the intellectuals. Sex was publicly discussed more openly and freely than ever before (Allen 1931, 118-121). William L. O'Neill asserts that in America, "the 1920s, not the 1960s was the time of the greatest movement toward permissive sexual behavior" (O'Neill 1969, 300).

Major league baseball's popularity, stimulated significantly by the conclusion of World War I (the National and American leagues had been formed in 1876 and 1900, respectively), rebounded from just over 3 million in total attendance for 1918 to over 6.5 million for 1919 and over 9 million the following year (Reichler 1962, 238 & 240).

The year 1919 held special significance for eight of the Chicago White Sox players and for baseball fans throughout the nation. Allegedly, eight players on the White Sox received money to lose the World Series to the Cincinnati Reds. Even though the eight were formally acquitted in court, all eight were subsequently banished from baseball for life by Judge Kenesaw Mountain Landis in 1920. The incident served to highlight a long history of graft, corruption, and illegal betting that had been a problem in baseball even prior to the formation of the leagues.

Some critics feared the scandal would destroy the popularity of the nation's pastime. Ultimately, however, the "Black Sox" scandal, as it became known, had little impact upon the game's popularity. Some historians feel the impact of the scandal was negligible due to the contributions of Babe Ruth and Judge Landis and because the scandal was so typical of the corruption that took place in theRoaring Twenties. Many fans did not find the scandal to be extraordinary (Lucas and Smith 1978, 318).

One of the by-products of the scandal was the creation of a caricature of the rural baseball hero. The characteristics of this hero would serve as the basis for the prototype of the back-woods sports hero for years to come. The real player from whom the rural baseball hero myth grew was Joe Jackson. Jackson was one of the infamous Chicago White Sox eight. He was the legendary "Shoeless" Joe Jackson of whom a young news boy, upon reading the headlines reporting the scandal, reportedly pleaded to Joe to, "Say it ain't so, Joe" (*New York Times,* December 1951). "Jackson was a 6-foot-1, 200 pound, unlettered South Carolina hillbilly who some have called the greatest natural ballplayer that ever lived" (*New York Times*, March 1951). Allegedly, Joe, who played nine full seasons in the major leagues, could neither read nor write and received the nickname "Shoeless" as a result of playing sans shoes in a minor league game after his newly acquired baseball spikes gave him sore feet. Jackson was a lifetime .356 hitter which is third only to Rogers Hornsby's .358 and Ty Cobb's .368. Even Cobb marveled at the greatness of Jackson's ability. According to Cobb,

> The finest natural hitter who ever lived was Shoeless Joe Jackson. He never gave batting the scientific study I gave it. He just swung. If he'd had my knowledge of the art, his averages would have been phenomenal (*New York Times*, March 1951).

Jackson's biographical data are important because many of his characteristics were later transformed into the Hollywood film versions of the stereotypic baseball player.

Historically, however, it has been Babe Ruth who has most frequently been referred to as the greatest baseball player that ever lived. It was George Herman "Babe" Ruth, the "Sultan of Swat," and Judge Landis, who ultimately emerged as the true heroes of baseball. Together they rescued the nation's pastime from the scandalous events of 1919.

> Landis and Ruth restored integrity and flare to baseball. Baseball, it seemed, had to have the appearance of purity demanded of a national pastime (Lucas and Smith 1978, 312).

Landis was appointed the first commissioner of major league baseball early in 1920. One of the very first items of business on Landis' agenda was the adoption of a livelier ball that permanently and dramatically changed the game of baseball from a game that emphasized strategy to one that emphasized power and the home run (*The Baseball Encyclopedia* 1969, 14).

The adoption of the livelier ball helped Babe Ruth hit 54 homeruns in 1920 after establishing the major league record at 29 just one year before. Babe Ruth became synonymous with baseball. In the twenties, "no one was more persistently popular, not even Lindbergh" (Smelzer 1975, 299). He was popular, not only for his athletic prowess but also because of his approach to life. Perhaps more than any other public person, Ruth symbolized a nation bent on enjoying life. "He fit the image of what a highly paid ballplayer ought to be and if he didn't really fit, the people wished to believe any legend that would shape the image" (Smelzer 1975, 299). Babe Ruth was *the* baseball story throughout the Roaring Twenties.

But the vision of eternal prosperity that was charateristic of the return to "normalcy" during the Roaring Twenties came to a screeching halt on an October night in 1929 when the stock market came crashing down, taking with it the hopes and dreams of many urban Americans. By the end of 1930, six million workers were unemployed. Pensions, retirement funds, homes, and countless other valuable possessions were lost.

Probably the most profound effect that resulted from the sudden economic crash was the nationwide psychological depression that afflicted many Americans. Apathy replaced activism even in the once hot arena of morality. Long dresses and skirts came back, bobbed hair was out, waist-lines could once again be noticed on women of fashion, and the "alarming" sex talk quickly became passé (Allen 1931, 387).

Hoover, fearing that Americans would lose their sense of "rugged individualism," refused to institute wide sweeping government programs that would alleviate some of the economic hardships that American families continued to suffer (Allen 1940, 38). Since the days of the pioneers, Americans had prided themselves on being able to survive through individual efforts.

But because of all the changes in American lifestyles produced during the twenties, it was almost impossible for urbanites to return to the days of self-reliance (Caughey and May 1964, 511). The sudden changes in prosperity, the conflicts that grew out of the moral and ethical contradictions, the corruption that continued to spread and feed off of the Depression, and the presence of extremely wealthy citizens in the midst of the growing poverty made for a chaotic and confused American public in the Depression era.

The Films

In the midst of this uncertainty came the first current of baseball films, covering the period from 1929 to 1935. The first film produced in this period, *Fast Company* (1929), a film adapted from a stage play of the same name by Ring Lardner and George M. Cohan, was the only film in this period released prior to the Crash. The remaining films, *They Learned About Women* (1930), *Hot Curves* (1930), *Fireman, Save My Child* (1932), *Elmer the Great* (1933), *Swell-Head* (1935), and *Alibi Ike* (1935) were released after the Crash.

Even though *Fast Company* was released prior to the Crash, the characteristics of the protagonist and the story of the film seem to be very similar to other films in this period. In fact, *Fast Company* was reworked and released as *Elmer the Great*. Some changes made in the remake appear to be reflective of the changes that were taking place in the greater society. According to the film review in *Sports Films* (1987) for *Fast Company*,

> Elmer Kane is a small-town baseball hero turned major leaguer with the Yankees. He's hopelessly in love with a vaudeville star who won't give him a tumble (Zucker and Babich 1987, 18).

In *Elmer the Great*, Elmer is a small-town baseball player hero playing for the Chicago Cubs,[1] and he is in love with a wholesome hometown girl who operates the local general store.

The fact that Elmer is a home run hitter for the Yankees in 1927 is no doubt meant to capitalize upon the adulation and popularity of Babe Ruth, who in 1927 hit 60 home runs in one season and in 1928 hit 3 home runs in the fourth and final game of the World Series. Elmer remains a home run hitter in the 1933 film probably due to Ruth's continued popularity, even though Jimmie Foxx of the Philadelphia Athletics outhit Ruth and led the American League with fifty-eight home runs in 1932.

The most noteworthy change that occurred from the original to the remake is the change in the woman Elmer is in love with in the two films. In *Fast Company*, the main woman in Elmer's life is a vaudeville star, a woman of the city. This would seem to be consistent with the popular urban attitudes of the Roaring Twenties. At a time when Americans were still riding the crest of prosperity, she represents all the attraction and fun associated with urban life.

However, in *Elmer the Great*, Elmer's dream girl is from a small town. She runs the store where Elmer works and encourages him to go to the big city to seek his fame and fortune. It is significant that in *Elmer the Great*, released after the crash, this female character reflects values that are predominantly associated with the more traditional values of rural America rather than the city. This is probably reflective of the distrust and confusion that many people had for the city during the Depression.

The films of this era share a good deal of commonality. The appearance of gamblers, the protagonist hailing from rural or small-town America, the protagonist being distracted from his game by a woman, and the protagonist winning the heart strings of his favorite girl after he wins the World Series are all typical scenarios for films of this period. It is difficult to generalize, in any detail, what some of the films in this initial era are about since I was able to view only the three Warner Bros. productions and since the plot summaries of the remaining films, taken from *Sports Films* and *The Motion Picture Guide*, are somewhat sketchy. However, based on the plot summaries and the film viewings, all of the films in this period share the above characteristics.

According to *The Motion Picture Guide*, the next film in this period after *Fast Company, They Learned About Women* (1930), was remade into *Take Me Out to the Ball Game* in 1949 and starred Gene Kelly and Frank Sinatra. *Take Me Out to the Ball Game,* a relatively popular film in 1949, was viewed as part of the research for this study. It is assumed that *They Learned About Women* is generally similar to the remake. The film depicts two male vaudeville stars, presumably urbanites, who become baseball stars in the spring. One protagonist prefers baseball, has associations with crooked gamblers, and falls in love with a woman who also appears to be a vaudeville star. He eventually marries her after his team wins the World Series. The other protagonist prefers vaudeville, falls in love with a more wholesome and more traditional urban woman, and is also married after the World Series. The gamblers attempt to keep the protagonist's team from winning the World Series.

The next film released in 1930 is entitled *Hot Curves*. According to Zucker and Babich:

> In this early talkie, it's the vamp . . . who turns the head of baseball star Jim Dolan. Soda Jerk Rubin, who becomes one of the key players for the Pittsburgh Cougars, helps bring his pal to his senses in time to win the big game (Zucker and Babich 1987, 23).

The vamp is the woman who saps the strength and/or money of the baseball hero and who usually gets "what is coming to her" by the end of the film (Zucker and Babich 1987, 5). This scenario is repeated frequently throughout this film era.

The last film in this era, *Swell-Head* (1935) was unavailable for viewing. This film does not appear in *Sports Films* or *The New York Times* reviews. *The Motion Picture Guide* says *Swell-Head* is an

> Overly tacky, stupid story about an egomaniacal baseball player who comes down to earth after being hit by a fast ball in the head. Apparently the pitch knocked some sense into him and the causes of his problems out of the way (Nash and Ross 1986, 3243).

There does not seem to be enough information in this summary to permit an accurate evaluation.

As previously stated, with the information that is available on these films, generalizations about them must be made with a degree of caution. However, I contend that the three Warner Bros. films viewed from this period do have elements of each of the non-viewed films in them and therefore can be considered to be representative of this film era. And so, the focus of this initial baseball film period will center on the three Warner Bros. productions: *Fireman, Save My Child; Elmer the Great*; and *Alibi Ike*.

Comic actor, Joe E. Brown, himself a former professional baseball player, stars in all three films. Brown was a popular film actor and highly valued by Warner Bros. during this period. Frank Nugent, writing in *The New York Times* in 1935, asserted that "Joe E. Brown is as important to Warner Bros. as Garbo is to Metro and Shirley Temple is to Fox" (Nugent 1935, 22).

Fireman, Save My Child (1932), which has very little to do with firemen saving children, was the first of the Warner Bros. baseball films. The film opens with a musical rendition of "Take Me Out to the Ball Game" and Smokey Joe Grant (Joe E. Brown) pitching for the Rosedale Fire Department's baseball team. The opposing team is the Orchid Lumber baseball team. The game is apparently the capstone event of the Rosedale Fourth of July Festival. The game is temporarily delayed by the unexpected burning of the Rosedale Sauerkraut Factory. Upon hearing the sound of the fire alarm, Grant drops everything at the baseball game and rushes to the scene of the fire. After a comic scene in which the kraut factory burns down, Grant returns to the festival to find everyone patiently awaiting his arrival. They have not moved from their pre-fire alarm positions. Grant throws one pitch and the game is over.

Young boys who are in attendance at the game follow Grant to his home and hang out under his window shouting questions about baseball as they argue about his statistics. "Is it hard to pitch?" one youngster asks Grant. He responds, "Not for a fellow with a natural curve like I." The grammar may be incorrect, but the message seems clear enough: Smokey Joe may not be educated, but he does have a natural gift as a baseball pitcher.

When a telegram comes from the St. Louis Cardinals inviting Grant to play professional baseball, he is encouraged by his girlfriend, Sally Toby (Evalyn Knapp), to take the offer as a way of achieving success. The implication is that there are limited opportunities for success in Rosedale and that true success stories are lived out in the big city. Grant is reluctant to leave Rosedale. He does not see playing baseball as anything more than a game and responds, "I ain't never gonna take baseball serious." After more discussion, however, Grant is convinced that by taking the job with the Cardinals, he would be provided with an opportunity to market his fire extinguisher invention that he has been struggling to perfect. His extinguisher is a ball composed of various chemicals that extinguishes a fire upon impact.

He arrives in St. Louis and is greeted with an icy reception from his wise-cracking, big city teammates who perceive him as a country bumpkin or what film critic Andre Sennewald calls "a rustic simpleton" (Sennewald 1932, 25). After watching Grant warm up in practice, Pop Bedlam (Guy Kibbee), a short, squatty manager says, "If that boy's heart was in baseball, he'd be the greatest pitcher in his generation." Another teammate cracks, "He'd rather pitch hay." Bedlam quickly growls, "I tell you, he's the greatest natural pitcher in the league." Later Bedlam tells the team, "If the rest of you could play ball like that cornfed boy, I'd be payin' off the mortgage with the pennant money right now."

Even though Grant's teammates ridicule him and he becomes the brunt of their practical jokes, his journey from the small town to the big city is romanticized in the film. He is seen as a character who possesses energy, optimism, honesty, and a school-boy naiveté, who manages to succeed even in the midst of the wise-guy, street-smart, urban atmosphere.

Several city people whom Grant encounters seem to be on the take or planning to con someone. In this environment, where honesty is a personality trait that is laughed at rather than revered, Grant becomes easy prey for even the smallest sting. But, in spite of the negative treatment from his peers and the misfortunes he encounters, Grant remains optimistic and confident. He is self-assured as he continues to out-perform his peers on the baseball field and gains the attention of various fans including an attractive baseball "groupie" named June Farnum (Lilian Bond).

It is made clear early in the film that Grant is uncomfortable and awkward around attractive women. For example, prior to his acceptance of the St. Louis offer, he almost forgets to ask Sally if she will be waiting for him when he comes back from St. Louis. When he does ask, she responds

Evalyn Knapp, Joe E. Brown, Fireman Save My Child *(1932). Photo courtesy of the Museum of Modern Art Film Archives, N.Y.*

with "You know I will Joe, but thanks for asking." Joe replies, "Awww, that's alright," as he looks down at the ground.

Another example of his awkwardness occurs after he joins the Cardinals and is traveling with them on the train. He is duped by two teammates into thinking that June is especially attracted to him, when, in fact, she sees Joe as a perfect mark for her get-rich-quick schemes. June is pretty, blonde-haired, and a girl of questionable morals. Joe is not smart enough or assertive enough to resist her advances, even though Sally loyally waits back home. Early in their relationship, June remarks that she is surprised that he has not talked about his baseball skills, and he responds, "If a man's a bigshot, he don't have to tell nobody. Take me for instance." June cracks back with, "Just give me time."

Under the pretense that she can help him find someone to market his fireball, June persuades Joe that he needs an agent and therefore must pay her to find one. Eventually, June completely drains Joe's Rosedale bank account and, at the same time, convinces him that they are engaged. Upon hearing June's announcement of their engagement, Joe reacts with "We are?" He seems totally out of his element with June.

Joe has been wiring Sally to make withdrawals from the Rosedale bank for him. After she sees that he has spent all his savings and because he has not answered any of her letters (Joe's manager has not given him any of Sally's letters, thinking that they might distract him), she plans a trip to St. Louis. Meanwhile, Joe tells June about Sally by saying "She's different from you. She's kinda shy, sweet, helpless like, you know the kind of girl that appeals to a big strong fella like I." He does not seem to understand why this statement upsets June.

When June and Sally finally meet in Joe's apartment, June berates Sally's small-town life style by saying, "It must be just too exciting to live in a small town, nothing to do but look after the cows and the chickens." June follows this statement by announcing to Sally her engagement to Joe. June turns to Joe and sarcastically says, "Let's get some weenies and visit Rosedale on our honeymoon." Joe is dumbfounded and does not know what to do to control the situation other than to say "I'm starved. Anybody care for a banana?" Sally abruptly departs.

Later, as he writes a letter to Sally that is intended to explain the situation, he mutters to himself, "A man needs a woman to take care of his cold and other things." Again his attempts at resolving the conflict that results from his ineptness at dealing with women only serves to further emphasize his incompetence.

Subsequently, Joe receives a telegram from a St. Louis bank notifying him that they are interested in financing his fireball extinguisher. He visits the bank, finds it closed, and is met by yet another big city, wise guy. This time it is the beat cop who asks, "What are you doing around here?" Joe responds, "Looking for the president." Instead of offering to lend assistance, the officer snaps back, "You're in the wrong town buddy. Better try Washington, D.C." Like a little boy caught up in trying to make a dream come true, Joe waits all night by the bank door for his once-in-a-lifetime shot at success. Finally, when the bank opens, the bank president gives him permission to sell his idea to the board. While he tries to persuade the bank's board that his fireball extinguisher is a worthy investment, the Cardinals are losing the World Series.

The final sequence of events in *Fireman, Save My Child* occurs in every one of the Warner Bros. films produced in this era. Brown, as the films' protagonist, arrives at the ball park at the last minute, scores the winning run, and thereby virtually single-handedly delivers the World Series to his team. He is the hero of the team and of baseball fans everywhere. However, none of the three Warner Bros. films ends here. In each film, *Fireman, Save My Child, Elmer the Great,* and *Alibi Ike,* Brown marries the wholesome and virtuous girl who represents the stereotypical and traditional American woman—faithful, understanding, and motherly. It is clear that Brown's reward for growing up, symbolized by his arrival at the top of his game and delivering the pennant to his team, is stability and responsibility in the form of the idealized woman, the woman who represents family and adulthood.

Elmer the Great (1933), the second Warner Bros. film of this first period, opens in a manner similar to *Fireman, Save My Child.* "Take Me Out to the Ball Game" is played once again as the audience sees an opening montage of shots of a frozen, sleepy, rural village called Gentryville, Indiana. A scout from the Chicago Cubs arrives in Gentryville to sign Elmer Kane (Joe E. Brown) to a major league contract.

The audience sees Elmer as an awkward and child-like character who marches to his own drum. As he gets out of bed at two o'clock in the afternoon, he puts two socks on the same foot. The scout calls Elmer on the phone and offers him the contract. Elmer rejects the scout's offer to play for the Cubs saying that he would rather stay in Gentryville and drive Nellie Poole's delivery truck. The scout is shocked at Elmer's response and inquires about Elmer's problems to Nellie Poole (Patricia Ellis). "Imagine a crossroads apple knocker high-hatin' the Chicago Cubs. . . . Say what kind of chump is he anyway?" the scout asks. Nellie replies, "He's one of the finest young men you'll ever meet."

Elmer's brother, Nick (Sterling Holloway), can not believe that Elmer is turning down a shot at the big leagues and says to his mother, "He may never get another chance like this in a thousand years. . . . Do you know what this means, ma?" Mother replies: "No, what does it mean, Elmer?" Elmer responds: "Don't mean a thing in the world to me, Ma, but it'll probably cost them the pennant. . . . Where's the pancakes? . . . I don't like any place I ain't never been." Nick continues to try to persuade "Ma" to use her influence on Elmer to change his mind. Nick makes references to Elmer being comparable to "The Babe" who is "the greatest hitter there ever was." Showing her ignorance of the city and of baseball, she responds to Nick, "Who is Babe Ruth?" Nick's reactions imply that Elmer is passing up every "normal" kid's dream of playing in the big leagues and he is not even aware of the magnitude of his decision.

Finally, Nellie Poole attempts to persuade Elmer to go to Chicago, as she states, "Why do you want to stay in a one-horse town like this when you got a chance to get out and be somebody? There's no future for you here." Similar to Sally's message in *Fireman, Save My Child,* the implication is that success lies in the city. But the message also indicates there are conflicting attitudes regarding the urban life versus the rural life among the Gentryville inhabitants. On one hand, the city represents the key to unlocking an individual's success. On the other hand, it represents the unknown, a life much different than Gentryville. Elmer reluctantly consents to go, and, at the same time decides to tell Nellie that the main reason he does not want to go is because he is in love with her. The confession appears to make him uneasy, and he avoids making eye contact with Nellie.

The similarities in character development in *Fireman* and *Elmer the Great* continue when Elmer gets to "the Bigs." The opening shot of spring training has Elmer asleep on a bench as a teammate shouts to another teammate, in reference to the sleeping Elmer, "Nature in the raw." His teammates trick him into fighting a "dummy" that they lay on top of him while he sleeps. Later, as the Cubs' manager and a player watch Elmer hit the baseball out of the park and through the scoreboard, the manager exclaims in awe: "The two best pitchers in baseball and he's hittin' it out without even tryin'." The player remains unimpressed and comments about Elmer's bragging: "Isn't he the paint job . . . fresh and wet from the bush league . . . a typical rookie." Once again the manager lectures the team to stay off Elmer's back. Another teammate comes to Elmer's defense when the players begin to voice their dissatisfaction with Elmer's presumptuous behavior: "Nah, Nah, Fellas. He's only sassy and ignorant. You can't blame a guy. He's had no education. He's just misfortunate." Again there are explicit references to the protagonist's lack of education and his natural abilities.

The Joe E. Brown character in this Ring Lardner remake is again the brunt of the city boys' jokes. In one sequence, he is taken to the hospital after sustaining an injury. At the hospital, he is tricked into talking into a medical instrument that he mistakenly believes is a microphone linked to a live radio broadcast. Upon discovering that he has been duped, he is quite embarrassed. His embarrassment arises from the nature of his message on the radio. Thinking that his words would reach his mother, he was sentimental and sincere in the bogus radio talk.

In spite of the conflicts Elmer experiences, he remains childlike and retains his optimistic attitude. He continues to be true to himself and his small-town values, which leads to difficulty and conflict with his teammates when they expect him to conform to their behavioral standards. Like a child, Elmer holds no grudges against his teammates and eventually forgets about any disagreements or problems he has with them.

Elmer, like Joe in *Fireman*, gets into trouble with his girlfriend back home when she unexpectedly comes to Chicago and finds out about Elmer's new girlfriend, an attractive blonde, urban woman named Evelyn Corey (Claire Dodd). Both women are upset that Elmer has neglected to tell either of them about the other. In disgust, they both reject him. Elmer is distraught and the audience knows that the situation could have easily been avoided if Elmer could only communicate more comfortably with women. He intends no harm to either woman and does not comprehend why they are so angry.

Meanwhile, Elmer's roommate gets into a spat with his wife on the telephone. He hangs up the phone and tells Elmer he's going to go get drunk to forget about his marital problems. Elmer, even though he does not drink, appears depressed after being rejected by both of his girlfriends and he decides to get drunk, too. "I'll go get drunk with ya. . . . I don't care what happens to me now," he says.

The speak-easy they visit is owned by gamblers and crooks. All of "the bosses boys" at the casino know the popular Elmer. Upon seeing him, one of them runs to the owner/manager of the casino and says "Guess who's drinkin' at the bar. . . . The guy that's got the World Series in his pocket."

The significance of this last statement and of several other similar references to Elmer's powerful ability in the film signify that Elmer is the one player who can single-handedly deliver the pennant to the Chicago Cubs. The statements imply that a particular individual on a baseball team, in this case Elmer, can make a critical difference to the success or failure of that team. The presence of this statement in baseball films seems to create a paradox since the game of baseball emphasizes the concept of the team. Yet the implication seems to be that although team work is necessary, strong leadership is also indispensable. In the Depression era, this concept seems to make sense. President Roosevelt was attempting to provide strong leadership and at the same time encourage every citizen to work together to get the nation on its feet again.

Subsequent events occurring at the speak-easy serve to reinforce the popularity of natural law over man-made/civil law. At the casino, Elmer is not aware that he is expected to pay real currency for the gambling tab he is accumulating by betting poker chips. He thinks he is playing for match sticks, "just like they do back home." He unwittingly signs an I.O.U. for $5,000 after which he is told that he can cover by losing the World Series. Offended by the suggestion that he throw the series, Elmer starts a fight with the casino owner and his gang and ends up in the hospital.

Elmer is angry and frustrated that he was taken advantage of by the gamblers, that his girlfriends did not give him a chance to explain, and that he has been tricked repeatedly by his teammates. (It is during this second trip to the hospital that Elmer finds out about the phony radio interview.) Elmer grabs the bogus microphone and announces:

> This is Elmer Kane speakin.' When I talked on the radio before I said I was gonna win the World Seriez.[2] Well I won't; I'm through. I'd die first 'for I'd played in it now! Let them smart

Joe E. Brown, Alibi Ike *(1935). Photo courtesy of the Museum of Modern Art Film Archives, N.Y.*

alecks and wise guys win the World Seriez by themselves, which they can't . . . the fresh stiffs.

As indicated earlier, Elmer has a change of heart and comes to the ball park just in time to deliver the game winning hit.

The Cubs owner, Colonel Moffitt (Berton Churchill), is hesitant to put Elmer into the game because he is suspicious of Elmer's relationship with the gamblers at the casino. The Cubs manager persuades the Colonel to allow Elmer to play. In the pouring rain and with the Cubs losing, Elmer hits the ball and scores the winning run by sliding head-first through the mud into home plate. The movie ends after Elmer marries Nellie and receives $5,000 from a bet he made on the Cubs winning the pennant. He uses the money to pay back his debt to the crooked gamblers.

The final film of this initial period is *Alibi Ike* (1935). The film begins much like the other two with "Take Me Out to the Ball Game" being played over a visual introduction of the stars of the film. This is followed by a montage of newspaper photos and headlines, including the announcement of Babe Ruth signing a contract.

The opening scene is spring training where the Chicago Cubs manager, Cap (William Frawley), is being told by the team's owner that this is his last season if he doesn't win. As Frawley looks at a rookie pitcher, he mumbles, "Bet I'll have to ring a cow bell to get him in off the field." Frawley continues to complain about the quality of his talent and how difficult it is to discover competent pitchers. As he complains, Frank X. Farrell (Joe E. Brown), alias Alibi Ike, crashes through the left field fence driving a noisy and unpredictable automobile.

This particular Brown character brags even more than Elmer Kane and although he's a pitcher, he brings his own bat to spring training. Frawley challenges Ike to step up to the plate to show how good he is. Ike obliges and hits the ball into his car which causes the car to start up and run unmanned, off the field.

Unlike the preceding two films, it is not absolutely clear where Ike is from. We are told he is from Sauk Centre, Iowa, but we see no visual cues regarding the nature of Sauk Centre. However, there are several visual and aural cues in the film that imply that Ike is either from a small town or rural America. Certainly his boyish character and backward nature are indications that his roots are not urban. A conversation that takes place between Ike and a few of his teammates at a pool hall illustrates this contention.

Ike: I never mess around much with girls.
Teammate: I see . . . just a woman hater, huh?
Ike: Sure . . . got no use for 'em. . . . I ain't so good at
             this game. . . . We don't play much pool at home.

Other indications that imply that Ike is not a city boy are incidences depicting Ike once again being used and manipulated by the people he comes into contact with.

For example, Ike goes to a jewelry store to buy an engagement ring for his girlfriend, Dolly Stevens (Olivia de Havilland). Ike is somewhat embarrassed by this activity and does not want to buy the ring while his teammates are around. He tries to lose them but cannot. His teammates know what he is trying to do even though he denies their allegations. They tell the store clerk that Ike is a bit crazy. The clerk, due to Ike's peculiar, backward behavior, believes them and reports him to the authorities.

Individualism is once again seen as a personality trait of the protagonist. Ike is noticeably different from almost everybody in this urban environment. Because of his constant bragging and alibi making, he alienates many of the people he comes into contact with, and in doing so, further isolates himself from the mainstream. He does, however, have an extraordinary ability as a baseball player and a great deal of confidence in that ability. For example, in an exhibition game, Ike pitches against the Yankees. He breezes through the first eight innings of the game. He appears to be in total control of the game into the ninth inning, as the Cubs have already scored nine runs.

Olivia de Havilland, Joe E. Brown, Alibi Ike *(1935). Photo courtesy of the Museum of Modern Art Film Archives, N.Y.*

He calls time-out and yells for his teammates to join him on the pitcher's mound. He instructs them to take a seat on the ground around him. He intentionally walks the bases full with nobody out. He intends to strike out the side but, instead, gives up a grand slam home run. He then proceeds to strike out the side and wins the game. It is his ability as a baseball player which makes up for his social inadequacies and earns him a place in the mainstream.

Another incident that depicts Ike's naiveté is a sequence that again involves gambling. A stranger, who introduces himself to Ike in the lobby of the team hotel as the president of the Young Men's High Ideals Club, petitions Ike to come over to the hotel room and give "the boys some pointers on clean living. . . . Some of them have had some problems with drinkin' and smokin'." When Ike hesitates, the stranger retorts "You're interested in health ain't 'cha? You'd like to see a young man keep his strength, don't [sic] cha?" Ike, admitting that both of these issues concern him, consents to go with the stranger.

The stranger's room is filled with smoke, and "the boys" are standing around drinking. They make jokes about the success stories for clean living that Ike shares with them. Ike is still not aware of what is really happening until the stranger offers to pay him to throw the game.

Ike refuses to throw the game, but bribe money is planted on him anyway. After the Cubs lose a game due to a shoddy performance by Ike (he actually played poorly because he and Dolly had a fight), the Cubs owner and Cap find the envelope with the money. Believing that Ike actually threw the game, they kick him off the team. He is unsuccessful in explaining to them what really happened and is subsequently kidnapped by the gang that attempted to buy him out.

Once again, Ike, as in the previous Warner Bros. films, escapes from his abductors, arrives at the park just in time, and hits and scores the winning run when he dives over the catcher's tag and onto home plate. His reward for this monumental feat is to be joined in marriage to Cap's sister-in-law, Dolly Stevens, who has remained loyal to Ike, in spite of his insensitive behavior toward her.

It should be apparent from the description provided of the three films in this first baseball film period that they are remarkably similar. Therefore, it seems appropriate for the discussion and analysis that follows to treat them as one and to acknowledge them as being representative films of this first film era. Each of the sets of competing values outlined earlier, regarding the natural hero and the civilized hero, is examined in the following analysis with respect to these Warner Bros. films.

Youth and Aging

There seems to be little doubt that in each of the films in this period, the protagonists' character is more closely linked to the natural hero than to the civilized hero regarding youth and aging. He is the innocent child in each film. He just wants to play baseball for fun. It is a game that Smokey Joe "ain't never gonna take serious."

The hero in this era is socially naive and child-like. He believes what people tell him. He openly trusts them and expects them to trust him. He is rarely aware of others attempts to use him and make fun of him. This tends to be a trait that is more commonly associated with a child's behavior rather than an adult's. His inability to view his environment from an adult's perspective is especially troublesome in the city where crooks, gamblers, and "fast-women" take advantage of his ignorance.

The heroes in this first film era are prone to display behavior that is moody and emotionally based rather than even-tempered, logical, and realistic. They tend to be optimistic and full of energy and spontaneity. All of these behaviors are exemplary behaviors of youth.

Another area that seems to be indicative of the hero's youthful nature is his lack of education. We know by his reactions to his environment, the things he says, and what others around him say, that he does not have a great deal of formal, practical education or experience with the city environment. Hence, many of the things he says and does are excused or at least excusable simply because he does not know any better, i.e., "He is just a kid." But his limited education also pertains to his lack of baseball training. The creators repeatedly tell the audience, in a variety of ways, that the heroes, Joe, Elmer, and Ike are naturally gifted. Like children, these heroes are unschooled and raw. The skills they possess are gifts of nature and not of training. Clearly, in regards to youth and aging, the hero in these early baseball films tends to possess youthful characteristics.

Women and Society

There appears to be only two kinds of women in these early films. The first is more conventional and agrarian. She possesses traditional values and performs traditional duties, e.g., she nurses the hero's ills, stays at home, manages the bank account, and above all else, remains loyal to the hero. She is "the kind of woman a man marries." The second dominant female type in the early baseball films is the urban female. She is generally cold, hard, deceptive, manipulative, and stunningly attractive. Both types of women, rural and urban, tend to be viewed by the coaches and other players in these films either as obstacles who stand in the way of the hero's success and subsequent adulthood, or as usurpers of the hero's strength, power, and ability.

The coaches' views of women explain why they do not want the hero to receive letters from his hometown girlfriends. The letters represent potential diversions to the hero's attention and concentration on baseball. The coaches' attitudes toward women in this instance are reflective of a popular and very traditional attitude that was spread by notable business moguls like Andrew Carnegie in speeches and writings in the late 1800s. In an address to a group of male students dated June 23, 1885, Carnegie said,

> Say each to yourself. My place is at the top. Make your vow that you will reach that position, with untarnished reputation, and make no other vow to distract your attention, except the very commendable one that when you are a member of the firm . . . you will form another partnership with the loveliest of her sex (Carnegie 1902, 4).

On the other hand, the protagonists in these films tend to see the good woman, the one he eventually marries, as the source of his strength and power. The coaches and players think they are doing the right thing by withholding the letters from home. Yet after the hero learns of the contents of the letters, his power is restored, and he begins to accomplish the extraordinary —for example, escaping from the confinement of the gamblers and scoring the winning run in the deciding game of the World Series.

In each film, the act of scoring the winning run represents the culmination of the protagonist's adulthood. It is not until he has struggled through the crises and events that lead to a well-adjusted adult life that he can collect the ultimate reward of adulthood: the responsibility of marriage. His accomplishments serve as testimonials to his readiness. When the hero tries to initiate a relationship with a woman prior to winning the World Series, he always meets negative consequences.

These films communicate two very different messages about the roles of women and society. One message depicts women as a necessary and integral part of the hero's life. Another message says that the women are obstacles who complicate his life and delay his entrance into the mainstream of the society he seeks to join. They are simultaneously the reward for success and the obstacle to success, desirable and yet undesirable. Similarly, the society they symbolize is both desirable and undesirable to the hero.

The hero has difficulty expressing his feelings for women and many of his attempts at being romantic are awkward and immature. In *Alibi Ike*, for example, Brown explains to the guys that he only asks Dolly to marry him because he feels sorry for the girl. When she overhears his statements, which were not intended to be malicious but rather to hide his discomfort with talking about his relationship with her around the guys, she temporarily exits his life and thereby delays his development.

The "good" women in these baseball films are emotionally stable, dependable, and loyal. By the end of the film they are still in love with the hero and still waiting to marry him in spite of his inconsiderate behavior. These women resemble mothers who patiently watch their irresponsible young boys grow into responsible men.

Society is not so much something that the protagonist in these films shuns or accepts as much as it is something he is not ready to handle. Lacking the required experience with the codes of conduct, language, and behavioral guidelines, he stands on the perimeter of society trying to get in but is repeatedly rejected by his peers and other established members of society. Generally, he does not fit; he is a loner. Left alone, he is free to display his individualism and his natural athletic abilities on the baseball field. His success on the diamond is his only avenue toward acceptance into the mainstream society. His teammates and society in general, because of their selfish desires to win the World Series, are eventually forced to accept him in spite of his social inadequacies.

Based upon the protagonist's discomfort in the presence of the good woman, his inability to successfully pursue a relationship with the good

woman prior to becoming the World Series hero, and his position as an outcast from the society, it seems appropriate to conclude that, regarding society
and women, the protagonist/hero in this early baseball film period tends to
lean toward natural hero tendencies. The films clearly show that the urban
world which the hero is attempting to join and that typically houses the civilized man and civilized society is much less virtuous than the natural-oriented
society from which the hero hails. The hero's success at the conclusion of the
film would seem to indicate that his value system is a necessary ingredient
for the success of the urban, more civilized society.

Politics and Law

The law of the city, which is equivalent to the law of "the big leagues,"
presents several problems for the protagonists in this early baseball film era.
Being unfamiliar with the official and unofficial codes of the big city results
in violations of these codes by the hero who typically abides by an internal,
more natural code. The gambling incident in *Elmer the Great* is a case in
point. Elmer does not think he should have to cover his gambling tab since he
thought he was just playing for fun. Nor does he believe that he should have
to prove to his team owner and manager that he is not on the take as a result
of the inadvertent gambling debt. Elmer knows intuitively that he would never allow himself to be bribed into losing a baseball game. His integrity would
not allow it. In his own mind, this is sufficient proof of his honesty and integrity. Elmer is unaware of the gambling history in baseball that justifies his
manager and owner being suspicious of him. The only history that he is familiar with is his own.

Generally, the baseball hero in this early period does not understand
that the unwritten laws of the urban society are based upon very different
principles and experiences than the grassroots, more personalized laws that
characterize his midwestern small-town experiences. In "the big leagues,"
people can and often do take advantage of the unlearned and inexperienced.
Typically, the criminals operate within the limits of the official law or at least
within the limits of the inability of the official law to be enforced. Concepts
of innate goodness seem to have little relevance for the inhabitants of the big
city of Hollywood's early baseball movies. The films' creators reserve the
characterizations of innate goodness for the natural hero who is not a product
of the city. Through the natural hero, goodness eventually triumphs.

The hero's natural athletic ability is explicitly championed in all of
these films. As indicated previously, there are several aural and visual references in these early films that speak to the esteem and awe that are afforded
an athlete with natural ability. These references symbolize the value of the

hero's internalized or natural behaviors. The hero's characterizations in this film era seem to be consistent with the behavioral tendencies of those associated with the natural hero outlined earlier in this work. According to Ray, the natural hero tends to isolate himself from the mainstream of society and build an individually meaningful world around family and friends (Ray 1985, 61). The hero decides to accept a major league contract to play baseball in *Fireman, Save My Child* and *Elmer the Great* not because of the prestige and financial reward that are certain to follow but because the people he values in his hometown think that accepting the contract is important. In an effort to please these people, he accepts the contract because he believes pleasing his small circle of family and friends is the natural thing to do. Therefore his acceptance is based upon friendship and love and not success or financial gain.

Like the child that he represents, the early baseball film hero feels no compulsion to change from his familiar and comfortable surroundings. At the same time, his acceptance of the major league contract and his subsequent move into the large city is representative of a natural progression in the chain of events that leads to his adulthood.

It seems reasonable to conclude that the hero of this initial baseball film era tends to be characterized by a natural code of conduct more than a civilized code. It is also apparent that the values of individualism, youth, and the laws of nature are the prominent values for the baseball hero of this period.

Conclusion

By virtue of the fact that each film ends with the baseball hero marrying the woman who most closely subscribes to the values of the traditional woman and who is symbolically the foundation of society and family, it seems appropriate to conclude that the films portray the value of the traditional marriage/family institution as paramount to the hero's success. Hence, there seems to be two distinctly different value messages in these films. Generally, the films romanticize and praise the natural hero's value system, yet with the baseball hero's marriage at the end of each film, the message is clearly one that reinforces the civilized hero value system. The necessity for the final act in these films should be obvious. As Ray asserts in his analysis of Hollywood films:

> Movies that refused to resolve contradictory myths typically found themselves without the large audiences expected by the industry; as a result, directors of such films found themselves without chances to work . . . Dramatization of the irresolvable conflict between American myths of success (celebrating energy and ambition) and of the simple life (warning that power and wealth corrupt) made audiences uneasy (Ray 1985, 57).

An additional rationale for the resolution of the competing value systems provided by the baseball hero's marriage becomes apparent when the films are placed in historical context. It would have been impractical and self-deprecating for filmmakers, during the Depression era, to create films that would trigger additional and unwanted conflict and anxiety within their predominantly urban audiences regarding urban values. Films that extolled the virtues of individualism, youth, and nature to the exclusion of the collective society, the experience of age, and the civilized codes of society would only add to the psychological ills of a nation already bent on the brink of disaster.

These three Warner Bros. films most certainly provided their audiences with a diversion from the miseries of the Depression; and, at the same time, they provided a sense of hope: a nostalgic longing for the "good ole' days." Yet they are consistent with a sense of hope for a brighter tomorrow. While the films may be commenting on the need to maintain the traditional perspective on the importance of our nation's basic institutions and the importance of cooperation, they were simultaneously commenting upon the necessity of strong individuals in our society to come forward and make a difference in overcoming adversity.

It is noteworthy here to point out some historical issues that these films either avoided addressing directly or addressed in a subtle fashion, as a sort of subtext. Three issues—gambling, prohibition, and the Depression—fall into this category and deserve some comment.

Gambling has long been a part of sports activities. Baseball is no exception. David Voigt reports in *American Baseball* that in the 1860s baseball betting was so common an event that most respectable clubs sold out for the benefit of gamblers (Voigt 1966, 16). As already pointed out in this work, the baseball gambling scandal of 1919 which forever branded the Chicago White Sox as the "Black Sox" is a significant example of the seriousness of the gambling problem in baseball.

Gambling or betting on baseball is mentioned in every one of the three Warner Bros. films in this era, and according to *Sports Films* and *The Motion Picture Guide*, at least two of the other non-Warner Bros. films have gambling subtexts. However, the films' creators make a distinction between two levels of wagering. They seem to assert that on a small level, gambling is fun and even part of the game, but on a larger, more professional level, it is taboo. Not until *Alibi Ike*, when the Chicago Cubs owner asserts to his manager the importance of "keeping the gambling element out of baseball," is there an attempt by these baseball filmmakers to "take a stand on the issue."

In *Alibi Ike*, the two different attitudes about gambling can be observed. Late in the film, a young boy approaches Ike and tells him how much Ike's World Series play means to him. "I got my bicycle bet on that game," whines the boy. Ike smiles and assures the lad that he will play well in the game and makes no comment about the boy's gambling, apparently lending his acceptance to gambling on this level. It is revealed later in the film that the youth is actually an employee of the leader of the gang that is attempting to buy Ike's services. Hence, gambling is ultimately associated with the criminal element. Yet, it is still clear that at least Ike and, presumably, others like him see nothing wrong with small-scale betting.

Further evidence of small-scale betting on baseball being approved by the creators and the audience is found in *Fireman, Save My Child*. The fire chief, who accompanies the fire trucks that answer the fire alarm at the bank where Smokey Joe Grant has started a fire, recognizes Grant. The fire chief petitions him to play: "Say Mr. Grant, I bet $50 on St. Louis today . . . tell you what I'll do . . . you win that game for me and I'll make you an honorary battalion chief with a hat and everything." Again, the message seems clear, especially considering that it is coming from the fire chief; small-scale gambling is acceptable.

A final example of the gambling issue is found in *Elmer the Great*. It has already been established here that a gambling casino was the scene of Elmer's demise after he was unable to resolve his problem of having two girlfriends. The casino is operated by the criminal element. But we see baseball players and other people, dressed in suits and fancy dresses, gambling there. Therefore, it must be assumed that gambling, even though it is associated with people of questionable morals, is commonly accepted. In a later scene in *Elmer the Great*, Elmer himself bets $5,000 on the game that he plays in so that he can pay off the gamblers and another debtor.

Clearly, the filmmakers during this era are giving two different messages on the gambling issue. In one sense, they portray it as an illegal and unwanted activity, especially when it comes to baseball. Yet there seems to be little question that they also give their unofficial approval of gambling on a small scale or when it is done with the "proper" motivation. If this dual message was reflective of the general society, it is little wonder that authorities historically have had a difficult time enforcing anti-gambling rules in professional sports. The filmmakers seemed to be implicitly reinforcing the common practice and popularity of gambling.

Similarly, in the first two of the three films from this era, which were released prior to the repeal of prohibition, liquor and speak-easies are commonly seen but there is no explicit attempt to address the issue of prohibition. Implicitly, there seems to be little doubt, judging by the presence of alcohol and speak-easies in these films, that advocating the violation of prohibition laws presented few, if any, problems for the filmmakers. Apparently, the presence of speak-easies was so commonly accepted by filmgoers during this era that filmmakers did not worry about anxiety that might be caused by the presence of these illegal entertainment halls in their films. However, as is the case with gambling, the filmmakers did provide two contradictory messages regarding alcohol. While alcohol and speak-easies often appeared in these films, the films' hero was never depicted in a way that would imply that he favored the consumption of alcohol or attending a speak-easy. Conversely, only when Elmer seemingly hits the low ebb of his life does he resort to going to a speak-easy/casino to drink and to end his troubles. As already asserted, it was at this time that he began to get into trouble. Hence, the message implied is that alcohol consumption leads to negative consequences.

However, there are others in these films who do drink alcohol and attend speak-easies, yet do not suffer negative consequences. The filmmakers, once again, provide the audience with two seemingly incompatible sides of an important contemporary moral issue. They imply that either side of the issue is acceptable. However, through the hero's character, the filmmakers are stating that gambling and alcohol consumption are associated with evil values. This approach is consistent with their goal of appealing to the widest possible audience. By resolving the contradictions presented in the film in a manner that is compatible with the audience's popular beliefs, the filmmakers diminish the risk of creating anxiety in the audience. At the same time, they leave the door of change ajar, implying that the less popular side of the issue is acceptable, just in case the popular opinion regarding the issues of alcohol and gambling swings in the opposite direction.

The final issue that demands analysis and comment is the issue of the Depression. The Depression is not openly dealt with at all in these Depression era films. On the contrary, the films' creators give very little specific dating to these films. Babe Ruth is mentioned in *Elmer the Great* as already having been established as the greatest hitter of all times. Therefore, baseball fans and baseball historians can assume that the film could take place sometime after 1920, the year Ruth hit an unprecedented fifty-four homeruns. Other cues to the time in which the film is set must be derived from the uniform styles, type and quality of equipment, technology utilized in the film, automobiles, and other similar culturally dated artifacts. There are no dates on any of the newspaper headlines that frequently appear in several newspaper montage sequences in the films. There is no acknowledgment of the president of the United States, other foreign leaders, or the commissioner of baseball. But the viewer can clearly see that the automobiles, uniforms, and communication technologies utilized in the films belong to the thirties.

Presumably, Hollywood attempted to make the films look timeless in order to emphasize the perennial appeal historically attributed to baseball.[3] The film creators have intentionally avoided reminding the Depression era audience of their own predicament. The baseball film hero in this period complies with the traditional set of natural hero values that the audience brings to the film. These natural hero or outlaw hero values of youth, individualism, and nature as opposed to the civilized or official hero values were more closely aligned to the world that the audience romanticized about rather than the world that they actually lived in. It seems plausible that the values associated with the civilized hero were precisely the values that the Depression era baseball film audiences sought to avoid.

Even though the films do not explicitly comment upon the Depression, it is apparent that the implied message of the films is hope. According to Frederick Allen, hope was one of the intangible commodities that was running low during this period (Allen 1931, 394). The Warner Bros. heroes which represented the embodiment of what Allen calls the "old-fashioned American idealism—friendly, naive, and provincial" (Allen 1931, 229), gave viewers numerous occasions to laugh, and, by the end of each film, the hero had provided the audience with a small ray of hope.

Frank Nugent, writing in 1935 for *The New York Times,* commented on the appeal of *Alibi Ike,* saying it was a film

> That will first appeal to the Brown enthusiasts, second to the Lardner disciples, third to the followers of the national sport, and fourth to the rank and file of film-goers who think there is nothing like a harmless comedy to brighten the dull moments of a hot summer day (Nugent 1935, 22).

Nugent's comments are applicable to all of the baseball films of the period. The films in this period appeal to the child-like instincts and values that are so much a part of our national sport and, by extension, a part of all of us.

One other relevant observation to make about these early films is that they imply the need for a strong individual leader. They show that it is possible for one man to step forward and deliver the team, and, by logical extension, the country, to the promised land, the land of the World Series Championship. Yet these films also imply that the team is important and must offer its support, even when its members disagree or dislike the "Messiah" that is sent to them. The films of this initial baseball film period hint that individualism is more important than the team. However, with a minimum amount of reflection, it is clear that the films also suggest that the individual can accomplish very little without the other team members.

In the final analysis, Hollywood seems to have been indicating that the small-town values that were so much a part of traditional America and of the natural hero were values that needed to be revitalized and reinforced in the Depression era urban audiences if the city, as well as the nation, was going to survive the Depression. Without the influence of the natural hero's youth, individualism, and natural goodness, there would be no energy and no hope for the future. Yet it also seems clear that Hollywood was saying that the traditional institutions associated with the city, like law and order, education, and the family, also had to survive the Depression for the good of the majority—and for the good of Hollywood. Perhaps, it was hoped that the synthesis that resulted from combining the virtues of the natural hero with the urban environment would re-establish a social order that had the potential of saving America. Such a synthesis would certainly reflect a more provincial and isolated America that, in relation to the rest of the world, saw itself as a small community needing to take care of its own. The world view resulting from such a synthesis correlates well with the isolationism and socialistic programs that preceded World War II and the next baseball film era.

Notes

1. A pattern that is established in this film and seems to carry through many baseball films of the various periods is that in the films where the protagonist plays for a major league team, the team is frequently one that, in reality, played in the World Series within two years of the release of the film. For example, in *Fast Company*, Elmer plays for the New York Yankees who won the World Series in 1927 and 1928. In *Elmer the Great*, Elmer plays for the Chicago Cubs who won the National League Championship in 1932.

2. Spelled phonetically the way Elmer says it in the film.

3. It is interesting to note that in *Fireman, Save My Child,* Smokey Joe Grant was invited to join the St. Louis Cardinals. The movie was released the year after the Cardinals won the National League Pennant. *Elmer the Great* was released the year after the Chicago Cubs won the Pennant, and *Alibi Ike* was released the same year the Cubs won the Pennant. Both of the latter films had Joe E. Brown playing on the Chicago Cubs.

Pride of the Yankees:
The Baseball Film Biography Prototype

S even years separate the initial baseball film period that ended with *Alibi Ike* from the second that begins with *Pride of the Yankees* (1942). Within these seven years, the FDR administration attempted to cure the psychological and economic ills of the country with the New Deal, and World War II began for the United States on December 7, 1941 with the bombing of Pearl Harbor.

Prior to Pearl Harbor, American opinions were somewhat divided regarding whether or not the United States should enter the European conflict, initiated in 1939 with the German invasion and occupation of Poland (Hamby 1976, 21). However, Americans across the nation rallied around the flag after the attack on Pearl Harbor. Millions of young men either enlisted or were drafted into the various branches of the military to do battle in World War II. Many women, who had never before worked outside the home, joined the labor force to take up some of the void that was left by the men being called into combat (Hamby 1976, 87). For many of the troops overseas and for many of those on the home front, it was the movies that provided the necessary maintenance of morale. Jowett asserts:

> Once America was thrown into a full-scale war, the motion picture industry immediately started to do that which it did best, provide entertainment for the public. Only this time it had an even greater mission—to provide strong moral support in time of crisis (Jowett 1976, 306).

The United States Government did not force Hollywood producers to instill blatant propagandist messages upon American audiences through commercial films (Jowett 1976, 311). Yet patriotic messages, whether presented subtly in a baseball film or presented explicitly in one of the more than

40

one hundred war films released, were abundant in American films during this period.

On the heels of World War II came the second baseball film era which includes just the years 1942 and 1943. There were four baseball movies released in this two-year span: *It Happened in Flatbush* (1942), *Pride of the Yankees* (1942), *Moonlight in Havana* (1942), and *Ladies' Day* (1943). *It Happened in Flatbush* and *Pride of the Yankees* were released just a few weeks apart in the summer of 1942. Of the four films, *Pride of the Yankees* is by far the most noteworthy and the most popular, having earned Academy Award nominations in ten categories[1] and an academy award for Daniel Mandell's film editing.

The majority of the discussion for this second baseball film era is based primarily on the observations made from viewing *Pride of the Yankees*. One of the reasons for this focus is certainly due to the tremendous popularity and critical acclaim associated with the film. But an additional reason for the focus is due to the impact that *Pride of the Yankees* would have on the next baseball film era, when six out of the seventeen baseball films released were biographies.

Except for *Pride of the Yankees,* the baseball films of this era seem to be relatively obscure. The obscure pictures are somewhat noteworthy when viewed within the context of the social milieu of 1942. Hollywood had lost a very lucrative part of its revenue sources with the closing of the European and Asian film markets. Trying to capture what was left of foreign markets led to some Hollywood producers making films that were designed to be appealing to Latin American audiences.

> To attract Latin America, the only foreign market left following the closure of Europe, Carmen Miranda was imported to Hollywood and musical after musical was set in Brazil or Argentina or Costa Rica (Higham 1968, 10).

Both *Ladies' Day* and *Moonlight in Havana* have Latin American stars and Latin American themes.

Moonlight in Havana is a musical about an American baseball player, a catcher, who is in Havana, Cuba, for spring training and discovers that he has a potential career as a singer in William Frawley's night club.[2] *Ladies'Day* is a film that stars Eddie Albert and Mexican actress, Lupe Velez. Velez plays the role of a Latin movie actress who falls in love with Albert, the star pitcher of a major league team called the Brooklyn Sox. Velez's character is a Latin stereotype. She has a thick Spanish accent. She is loud and very temperamental.

Ladies' Day and *It Happened in Flatbush* depend on one of the tendencies that was noted in the first baseball film period. Both films revolve around the image of women as obstacles to the hero's success. *Ladies' Day* almost exclusively centers on the events that transpire as a result of the players' wives conspiring to keep Velez and Albert physically apart, even though they are married. Their actions are triggered by the fact that Albert has a history of going into a complete nose dive whenever a woman comes into his life. The team desperately wants to win the pennant, and everybody associated with the team knows that winning the pennant is impossible without Albert pitching at an optimal level. It seems clear that the producers of *Ladies' Day* intended to attract a female audience, hence the title, the predominance of women in the film, and the amount of screen time devoted to the relationships of the various women.

Most of the women in *Ladies' Day* are far more assertive and domineering than are the males. Max Baer, who plays a dopey catcher, is totally dominated by his wife, who is without question the real force behind the film. The predominance of women can probably be attributed to the fact that women populated the paid work force during the war, had more money to spend on films, and were more available than men. It made logical business sense to target the female viewer.

In *It Happened in Flatbush*, Lloyd Nolan, a former big leaguer buried in the bush leagues, is given his big chance when he is hired to manage the Brooklyn Dodgers. Things are going well for Nolan and the team until he falls in love with the team's majority stockholder, Carole Landis. As Nolan's involvement with Landis grows stronger, the team's slump deepens until the players unite to petition for Nolan's removal. Their action is enough to get Nolan's attention; he rededicates himself to the team, and they win the pennant (Zucker and Babich 1987, 24).

Ladies' Day and *It Happened in Flatbush* have one other noteworthy element in common. Both films are about a major league team that hails from Brooklyn, New York. After years of frustration that earned them the affectionate tag of "Dem Bums" (*Time* July 6, 1942, 81), the Brooklyn Dodgers finally won the National League Pennant in 1941, only to lose the World Series. Judging from the appearance of the St. Louis and Chicago teams in the earlier film period, immediately following pennant-winning seasons for those two teams, and by the presence of Brooklyn teams in two of the four films in this film period, it seems reasonable to conclude that the baseball film creators used familiar and popular team names from real major league teams to enhance the popularity of the film. Presumably, this might be true especially when a considerable amount of public sentiment and publicity associated with the club, as was the case with the Brooklyn Dodgers of 1941.[3]

Even though there are elements of each of the previously mentioned films in this second era that reflect the social climate, it is unquestionably the

Pride of the Yankees that best represents the 1942-43 baseball film period. It is "the" film of this era not only because of its tremendous popularity, when compared to all other baseball films, but also because it is a story about a particular baseball player who most appropriately embodies the moral standards, ethics, and popular values that Hollywood creators and the Roosevelt administration sought to exemplify and reinforce for the American audiences during this period of world strife. *Pride of the Yankees* is also significant because it is the first non-comedy baseball film released, and it is the first biography baseball film.

The Films

Pride of the Yankees was directed by Sam Wood, a director of other notable films such as *A Night at the Opera* (1935), *A Day at the Races* (1937), *Goodbye, Mr. Chips* (1939), and *King's Row* (1940). The film was produced by Samuel Goldwyn. According to Jay Nash, Goldwyn was initially reluctant to produce the film. When he did decide to produce it, he took some calculated risks.

> Goldwyn disregarded most of his potential audience. At the time women were not interested in baseball, baseball enthusiasts did not get much of a glimpse of the sport, and since the sport is strictly an American pastime, foreign sales would be curtailed (Nash and Ross 1986, 2454).

However, Jowett (Jowett 1976, 283) and Higham (Higham 1968, 10) assert that the amount of revenue from foreign sales was already drastically reduced by 1941. Therefore, it seems likely that by the time *Pride of the Yankees* was made, the foreign revenue factor was negligible in regards to Goldwyn's decision. It is also refutable that baseball is/was *strictly* an American pastime unless the consideration of America here extends to all of the Americas. Baseball was and is, in fact, very popular in Latin America, the major foreign market of American films during the war. Finally, the film that Goldwyn produced probably had a great deal of general appeal to women, as it was as much a love story as it was a baseball enthusiast's film. Therefore, Goldwyn's risks seem less risky than Nash indicates.

The film opens with a serious tone. Music is playing in the background as the following words appear on the screen:

> This is the story of a hero of the peaceful paths of everyday life. It is the story of a gentle young man who, in the full flower of his great fame, was a lesson in simplicity and modesty to the youth of America.

He faced death with that same valor and fortitude that has been displayed by thousands of Americans on far-flung fields of battle. He left behind him a memory of courage and devotion that will ever be an inspiration to all men. This is the story of Lou Gehrig (*Pride of the Yankees*).

Following these words, the music tempo changes to upbeat and the scene is a bustling large city thoroughfare around the turn of the twentieth century. A boy jumps off the back of an ice truck and races through the traffic to a sandlot baseball game that is taking place in a small vacant lot surrounded by large tenement houses.

The young boy, who identifies himself as Lou Gehrig, joins in the game. He looks proud and excited as he takes his turn at the plate. He swings at the first pitch delivered and hits it over the fence and through a nearby shopkeeper's storefront window. He is apprehended by a policeman and the shopkeeper and is taken home to his unemployed immigrant father.

Gehrig's mother is employed outside the home and has not yet arrived. The father looks uneasy and in a heavy German accent exclaims "I can't do anything without my wife." The mother eventually arrives, and Lou tells her that he is sorry and that he did not know he could hit that far. "What we break we pay for . . . baseball!" says Mrs. Gehrig as she pays for the window. She too has a heavy German accent.

Lou offers to quit school to help pay for damages. Mother Gehrig then goes into a long litany of how she wants him to be more than a janitor or a cook. She wants him to go to college, to be somebody, to be an engineer like his uncle Otto. "Maybe I'm not cut out to be an engineer," Lou asserts. "In this country," says Mama, "you can be anything you want to be."

There are several scenes that follow that serve to illustrate the closeness of the relationship between Lou (Gary Cooper) and his mother. He goes to college to study engineering, joins a fraternity, and turns down an offer to play with the Yankees, just to please his mother. At a fraternity dance an attractive young lady asks Lou if he always does what his mother wants. Lou responds, "Of course," as though there were no other response available.

Even though Lou turns down the initial offer from Sam Blake (Walter Brennan), the Yankee Scout, to play pro baseball, he is forced to reconsider when his mother becomes seriously ill. He secretly accepts the offer so that he can pay for her medical expenses.

At first, Lou and his father are able to keep the news of his new career away from Mother Gehrig. But when Lou gets promoted from the farm club to the Yankees, the news is in all the papers and Mrs. Gehrig finds out from the neighbors. She is distraught, disappointed, and infuriated that Lou has given up on his education. Lou protests, "You've never been to a ball

George Herman "Babe" Ruth, Gary Cooper, Pride of the Yankees *(1942). Photo courtesy of the Museum of Modern Art Film Archives, N.Y.*

game. Lots of people go. Men, women, and children." "You are good for nothing. All ballplayers are good for nothing. . . . A disgrace like that . . . that's why we come to America, a wonderful country where everyone has an equal chance?" scolds Mama Gehrig.

A montage of many scenes follow showing Lou sitting on the Yankee bench waiting to get into a game. He finally gets to play when the regular first baseman gets injured. As he leaves the dugout, Lou steps on the bats that are lying flat on the field in front of the dugout and falls flat on his face. Everybody in the stands laughs including Eleanor Twitchell (Teresa Wright), his future wife. Eleanor and Lou's courtship begins at a restaurant where they meet after the game.

Another noteworthy scene occurs on the train as the Yankees are "on the road." "Take Me Out to the Ball Game" plays in the background as Babe Ruth (Babe Ruth) enters the berth where the rest of the Yankees are playing cards and acting like a group of rowdy children. The Babe is sporting a new straw hat and makes it a point to tell the guys to leave it alone. When Babe turns his back, one of the players steals the new straw hat and passes it around. Each of them takes a turn biting chunks out of the brim. The hat gets passed to Gehrig. He is told he must take two bites in order to be accepted by the guys. Of course, Lou gets caught by an irate Babe Ruth. Two sportswriters traveling with the team begin to talk about the incident. One writer is the Yankee Scout, Sam Blake, and the other is Hank Hanneman (Dan Duryea).

> Hanneman: That Gehrig's the chump of all time, falling for a gag like that.
>
> Blake: Ah he doesn't know about gags.
>
> Hanneman: What does he know about Mr. Bones?
>
> Blake: Baseball.
>
> Hanneman: Ah, he's a detriment to any sport. He wakes up, brushes his teeth, hikes out to the ball park, hits the ball, hikes back to the hotel room, reads the funny papers, gargles, and goes to bed. That's personality? Humph.
>
> Blake: The best.
>
> Hanneman: A real hero.
>
> Blake: Let me tell you something about heroes, Hank. I've covered a lot of 'em. I'm tellin' you Gehrig is the best of 'em. No front page scandals, no daffy excitements. No hornpiping, but a guy who does his job and nothing else. He lives for his job. He gets a lot of fun out of it and fifty million other people get a lot of fun out of him, watchin him do something better than anybody else has ever done it before.
>
> Hanneman: You'd be right, Sam, if all baseball fans were as big boobs as Gehrig.
>
> Blake: They are . . . the same kind of boobs as Gehrig only without a batting eye. That's why I'm putting my money on Gehrig.

As Eleanor and Lou's relationship grows, Lou's thoughts are increasingly about Eleanor when he is on the road. As in the previous baseball film era, their relationship is depicted as somewhat of an obstacle to Lou's baseball playing. At one point before their relationship is consummated, Lou is shown blowing an easy play at first base after making eye contact with Eleanor, who is seated in the stands.

One sequence in the film seems to be an attempt on the part of the film's creators to rewrite a bit of baseball history (Babe Ruth's mythical called shot in the 1932 World Series), in order to further characterize Lou in the image of Blake's blue-collar ballplayer. Babe Ruth is seen at a hospital along side the bed of a frail boy named Billy. Babe presents Billy with a Babe Ruth autographed ball as reporters' flashbulbs light up the room. As the Babe exits Billy's room, he boastfully promises to hit Billy a home run to center field at today's game. Lou and Billy are alone in the room except for the unnoticed Sam Blake. Billy turns to Lou and asks him to add his name to the souvenir baseball.

Billy: I'd like to play baseball.
Lou: You'll play again Billy, you know there isn't anything you can't do if you try hard enough.
Billy: You think so?
Lou: Why sure.
Billy: Could you knock a home run for me this afternoon?
Lou: Why, you've already been promised one by, by Babe Ruth.
Billy: Could ya?
Lou: Well that's a pretty tall order. . . . Okay.
Billy: Could ya knock two homers?
Lou: Two homers in a World Series?

Babe Ruth and Lou Gehrig did, in fact, hit two home runs each in game number three of the 1932 World Series between the Chicago Cubs and the New York Yankees. Ruth's second home run of the game came in the fifth inning after taking two called strikes and a verbal thrashing from the Cub bench. As one story goes, the Babe pointed one finger in the direction of the Cubs pitcher, signaling that he had one strike remaining. Other accounts, including the one favored by the press, claimed that his gesture was a sign that he was going to hit a home run to center field (Sugar 1986, 72). Regardless, Babe hit the next pitch over the center field wall for the celebrated "called shot."

However, *The Pride of the Yankees* version of this particular game attempts to focus the audience's attention on the unceremonious efforts of Gehrig to fulfill his promise to the sick boy. The film plays out the sequence in dramatic fashion as the radio commentators play up Gehrig's last chance to fulfill his promise, which he does.

After the World Series, Eleanor and Lou decide to get married and go to New York to surprise Lou's family with the news. The following sequences depict Lou's mother and Eleanor's relationship as tense and unsettling. Lou's mother is aggressive and obstinate. Mrs. Gehrig and Eleanor argue about furniture, drapes, carpeting, and wallpaper for Lou and Eleanor's home. Mother Gehrig orders delivery on the merchandise that she likes in spite of Eleanor's objections. Lou intervenes in favor of Eleanor. When he finds Eleanor crying over the stove he explains that he has sent all the things that Mama ordered back to the stores.

> Eleanor: I hope you didn't hurt Mama's feelings.
> Lou: I probably did but she'll get over it. She'll have to. You can't run a baseball team with two captains nor a household with two bosses. There's only gonna be one boss in this house.

A significant portion of the remainder of the movie depicts Lou and Eleanor as having the "ideal" marriage. It is a marriage in which Eleanor supports virtually everything that Lou does. For example, Lou's father encourages the couple to take a honeymoon. Lou refuses because it would mean missing a game. He explains to his father that he has never missed a game and he is not going to start now that he is married. Eleanor supports his decision by half-seriously stating, "I'll divorce him if he does."

Another example of the film's depiction of the Gehrigs' ideal marriage takes place in a scene in which Sam Blake, who becomes one of their closest friends, arrives at the Gehrig home expecting to see Lou. Eleanor greets him and insists she does not know where Lou is but that Sam should not worry because, recently, Lou has been consistently late and frequently, and inexplicably, misses dinner. Eleanor leaves the room and Sam, suspecting that Lou may be having an affair, mutters "What will the fans think?" Then Blake says to Eleanor, in what seems like an attempt to ease his own conscience, that she doesn't know how lucky she is to have Lou, "Lou is true blue." Eleanor convinces Sam to join her as they cruise the neighborhood looking for Lou. She pulls up to a young boy's sandlot baseball game where Lou is the umpire. She laughs heartily as Sam realizes his suspicions were completely unfounded.

Repeatedly, there are scenes in which Eleanor and Lou are shown reaffirming their love and loyalty to each other. Eleanor keeps a scrapbook of all of Lou's accomplishments. Lou invites Eleanor to spring training rather than to "pal around with the team." Lou apologizes for never having taken Eleanor on a honeymoon, and she responds "We've never had anything else." Eleanor also talks about what she has given up to be with Lou. She asserts to Lou:

> Dad was right. I left my little world behind me. Baseball life is so different. Sort of a little world all by itself. You play it in the spring, summer, and fall and talk about it in the winter. You really eat, drink, and sleep it.

Thinking that she's grown tired of the life, Lou offers her an oppor-

Gary Cooper, Teresa Wright, Pride of the Yankees *(1942). Photo courtesy of the Museum of Modern Art Film Archives, N.Y.*

tunity to stay home but she adamantly refuses.

After several other lengthy scenes showing Lou and Eleanor laughing together, Lou discovers that he has something seriously wrong with him. He tries to brush aside whatever is ailing him, but he is unable to continue playing. Finally, he pulls himself out of a game after playing for the all-time record of 2,130 consecutive games. His disease is diagnosed as amytropic lateral sclerosis, now known as Lou Gehrig's disease. After the doctor performs a thorough physical examination, Lou petitions the doctor to "Tell it to me straight, Doc; is it three strikes?" The physician affirms Lou's suspicions, and Lou requests that the doctor not tell Eleanor. But Eleanor enters the room as Lou leaves and instinctively asks Sam Blake, "When is Lou going to die?"

Eleanor continues to support Lou and continues to find things to smile about. She escorts Lou to the field on Lou Gehrig day at Yankee Stadium. She stays behind on the ramp as Lou goes to the field to receive his awards which include a plaque that says "Don't quit." He then delivers his "thank you" speech:

I have been given fame and undeserved praise by the boys up

there behind the wire in the press box, my friends, the sportswriters. I have a mother and father who fought to give me health and a solid background in my youth. I have a companion for life who has shown me more courage than I have even. People all say that I've had a bad break but today, today I consider myself the luckiest man on the face of the earth. (*Pride of the Yankees*)

The movie ends as "player number four" walks away from the camera and down the dark ramp into Eleanor's waiting arms. The sound of applause fades into the closing music.

Youth and Aging

There are several elements in *Pride of the Yankees* to indicate that youth is once again the value that receives emphasis in this film period. The most significant examples of the youthful values depicted in this film are: (1) Lou's child-like innocence, behavior, and naiveté, similar to but not as extreme as the heroes in the previous film period; and (2) Lou and Eleanor's energetic marriage that was based on their devoted friendship. It should be mentioned here that in several incidents Lou's Yankee teammates are shown engaging in rowdy and boisterous behavior much like young teenage boys.

Lou is depicted as an honest and sensitive "boy-man" very early in the film. He wants to play ball so badly that he gives up nearly all his baseball cards for one chance to bat. He is so completely enthralled in his mammoth hit in the sandlot that he does not even realize what he has done nor the consequences that will most certainly follow. But immediately upon breaking the grocer's window, he offers to do whatever he possibly can to repay his mother, who has paid for the window. His mother tells him, it's not so much the money but the time he wastes playing baseball. She stresses the importance of education, and Lou promises to become an engineer.

Like a small boy, Lou continually seeks his mother's approval and affection. When Lou is asked to join the fraternity, he gives his fraternity pin to his mother, a further indication of a young boy's love for his mother.

As in the previous film period, the protagonist is inexperienced and awkward around women. Since he has no experiences on which to base his interaction with females, he communicates with them hesitantly but at the same time, he is open and honest, seemingly unaware of the risks or the consequences that might result.

Lou's character seems to vacillate from boy to man and man to boy throughout the film. Although he is unable to control his anger in an incident involving the teasing he receives from his fraternity brothers, he normally maintains total control of his temper.

Frequently, he exhibits natural hero traits and civilized hero traits simultaneously. A clear example of this occurs when his mother must go into the hospital and Lou makes the rather mature decision to quit college and to sign a contract with the Yankees to play baseball and thereby pay for the best medical care available for his mother. This decision seems reasonable until the boy in him takes over. In order not to disappoint his Mama, who wants him to go to college, he and his father conspire to keep the truth from her. The adult response to this situation would be to tell her exactly what he did and why he made the decision. Instead, Lou's decision seems child-like. He is naive enough to think that his domineering mother will not find out about the secret. Like a child, he does not give much thought to what she will do when she does find out.

Another example offered as testimony of Lou's child-like behavior takes place on one of the first dates Lou and Eleanor have. They begin a very formal evening by going to the fair. Lou is seen in his tuxedo, batting balls into a target and winning an arm load of cupie dolls for Eleanor. He is asked to leave the batting game because he is winning too much. He is subsequently distracted by another game. In this game a player takes an oversized and overweight sledgehammer and hurls it at a platform which in turn causes a weight to rise up in the air and ring a bell at the top of a pole. It is supposed to be a test of strength, but most everybody knows, including Eleanor, that it is as much a test of where the contestant hits the platform as it is strength. Lou sees a small man ring the bell, and he decides to try. But before Lou can test his skill, a larger man swings the hammer and the weight only goes about halfway up the pole. Lou thinks twice about playing, but Eleanor coaxes him to try. After a couple attempts, he succeeds in ringing the bell. This seems to symbolize how Lou uses the carnival games as a test of his virility and worthiness, much like an inexperienced and immature teenage boy might. Seen from this perspective, the more vigor and strength he has, the more cupie dolls he is capable of winning, and the more worthy he is of Eleanor's attention and affection.

Lou portrays boyish innocence, too, when he takes two bites out of the Babe's hat because a teammate tells him to do so. Later in the film, Lou again looks boyish when he falls over the bats in front of the dugout. In addition, this incident seems to be symbolic of Lou's "learning how to walk" in the major leagues.

Finally, Lou's actual record for having played in 2,130 consecutive games serves as a symbol of his everlasting youth. It also serves to underscore and emphasize the strength of this film, Lou as the image of the blue-collar man in the trenches.

The second significant category of youthful values depicted in *Pride of the Yankees* centers around the type of marriage Lou and Eleanor are shown to have. Their marriage seems more akin to an oath of friendship between two childhood friends than a match between two adults who have fallen in love. No less than three scenes show Eleanor and Lou laughing, wrestling, rolling around on the beach or on their living room floor. They throw roses and sand at each other and play tag. They accompany each other virtually everywhere. The only exception to this togetherness is when Lou is umpiring the little league game.

The youthful Gehrigs verbally express how much they enjoy each other's company and how their marriage has been one long honeymoon. The absence of children in their marriage might be an indication that the honeymoon statement is valid. They appear almost too young and too carefree to be saddled with the responsibility of a family. Their romantic behavior is representative of the behavior generally associated with an intimate relationship that is very young and new.

In this second film era, as in the previous film period, youth is valued over aging. However, in this second period, the dreams and visions of youth are offset by the reality and finality of death. In the beginning of the film, the audience is reminded with printed words that Gehrig's untimely death in the flower of his youth is similar to the untimely deaths served on the thousands of young men who died on the battlefields. It is perhaps a bit heavy-handed to suggest here that the hardships faced by Gehrig are similar to those faced by the nation's soldiers, but what is similiar in both situations is the courage of youth in the face of death. Furthermore, the film probably offered audience members some emotional consolation for the young men in their lives who made the ultimate sacrifice, fighting for their country's traditions and freedoms. The reality of the war was such that many young men were required to age well before their time. Because of the war, there was not time for them to experience the frivolity and irresponsibleness of youth. They had to contribute to the benefit of the greater society. That became more important than living out the dreams of youth.

Women and Society

Women seem to play a more important role in this second baseball film period than they did in the first. As has already been indicated, the film *Ladies' Day* was heavily populated with female characters who dominate the film's male characters. Traditional values and traditional women's roles seem to be valued in this period just as they were in the last. However, there is a major departure from the tendencies established in the previous era regarding the protagonist's position in society. In the first era, the natural hero tends to be on the outside of society and is not really accepted into the culture of the city and civilization until the end of the film. This does not appear to be the case here. Lou Gehrig seems ready to embrace the responsibilities of being a part of society and rarely, if ever, questions his life's path.

Unlike his counterpart in the initial film period, there is no need to achieve complete success prior to beginning a relationship with a woman. Entering college is equivalent to Lou entering adulthood. College appears to be the substitute for going out into the world and finding success. Lou is on the verge of manhood when he tells Myra (Virginia Gilmore), the girl at the fraternity dance, that he is not going to play baseball, the symbol of a child's game, because his mother wants him to be an engineer. The implication here is that good boys, of course, do what their Mamas want them to do and take on real jobs and responsibilities, especially in the land of opportunity.

Lou's mother is quite clearly the moral and economic strength of the family. Lou's father does not know what to do when the policeman and the grocer bring Lou home after he breaks the grocer's window at the beginning of the film. The role of the father is established here as being weak. It is Mother Gehrig who establishes good strong morals and supports the family, just as it must have been the mother in the greater American society during the war years who provided these elements for many American families when the men were gone. Lou is taught by his mother to appreciate the "Great American Society," and the promise that in this country you can be anything you want to be if you work hard enough.

It is clear that the mother and father are immigrants and that the mother works steadily to support the family. Mother Gehrig is the source of Lou's work ethic, honesty, and courage. It is significant that the city in *Pride of the Yankees,* unlike the one portrayed in the first period, does not house gamblers, crooks, or vamps. Even the son of German immigrants can get an education in this city. The traits that are valued here are very explicitly pro status quo and Lou wants to be a part of it from the start.

The message of the film becomes even clearer, regarding the change in the hero from the first film period, when one of the events of the film is compared to reality. In the film, shortly after Eleanor and Lou meet they are eagerly married. They are depicted as two young people who are ready to embrace the institution of marriage and become part of civilized society. In reality, Lou and Eleanor dated for seven years before they finally got married, and then, only after much pressure from family and friends (*Current Biography* 1940, 331). Eleanor already owned apartments in Chicago, and Lou, who was thirty years old, had already been in the majors for ten years.

In sequence after sequence, Eleanor is depicted as the loyal, wholesome woman whose primary duties are to maintain a scrapbook of all of Lou's achievements and to support him whenever he needs her support. She basically has no other life apart from Lou. He frequently tells her how important her support has been to him, and he also communicates to her that he knows following him around has not been easy. In return for her loyalty and dependability, Lou gives his loyalty and dependability. He is never seen to take a drink, smoke, be unfaithful, or even associate with his teammates, other than on the field or on the team train.

Loyalty and dependability are traits valued in the civilized hero's world. Lou gives his teammates his loyalty and dependability on the field. He is there every game for 2,130 consecutive games. He spent his entire baseball career with the Yankees. No other team ever had his allegiance. Gehrig is the embodiment of the model citizen in 1942. This is quite evident in the "called home run" sequence that in reality centered around Babe Ruth.

The audience sees the boisterous Babe Ruth repeatedly smiling and posing for the reporter's cameras as they take pictures of him signing the bedridden boy's baseball. Ruth brags about his abilities as he laughs aloud and tells the boy how he will hit him a home run. In contrast, Lou is shy and more reserved as the boy asks him to sign the baseball too. Then without reporters' interpretations or any other fanfare, the audience sees Lou reluctantly promise to hit two home runs if the boy will promise to walk out of the hospital on his own power some day. Unlike Ruth, who does his "thing" with the flash, flair, and energy of the twenties, Gehrig is the blue-collar worker of the Depression era, the man in the trenches on the front lines during World War II. Sam Blake's testimony to Hanneman serves to underscore this point.

According to Sam, Lou is exactly the kind of hero that society wants and needs. He is the model citizen and the model hero. In 1942, one year after Gehrig's death, he is portrayed as the quintessential American Hero.

Politics and Law

There is no question that this film period reflects an attitude that values working within the law to accomplish the goals of society.[4] The tone for this law and order film is established early on with the broken window scene. The policeman who apprehends Lou is almost apologetic for having to carry out his duties. In addition, there are two other incidents in this film where policemen appear. Neither time are they depicted as incompetent, corrupt, or impersonal. Contrary to the natural hero tendency that views the law as ineffective and impersonal, the law in *Pride of the Yankees* is seen as extremely friendly.

In another scene where law enforcement officers appear, Lou is violating the law as he speeds in his car to be on time for a baseball game. In a third scene involving the law, Lou is suspected of trespassing. He is caught "prowling" around Eleanor's family estate early in the morning as he tries to build up enough courage to ask Eleanor to marry him. In each instance, once Lou tells the police officers who he is and why he is doing what he is doing, he is assisted by them and is subsequently excused. In all three of the incidents involving the police, the message seems to be that honesty is rewarded even when the law is broken, and that the law enforcement agents are just and understanding. The only time in the film that Lou attempts to take the law into his own hands, he ends up looking foolish. The reference here is to the fraternity house scene in which he fights with his fraternity brothers.

By the end of the film, Lou's character is a complete model of an American hero who lives by the laws of society but who can also adapt to the laws of nature. He accepts the doctor's fatal prognosis just as he would accept a called third strike by the umpire. He does not think that he has been dealt a bad break but rather, with all that he has and all that he has accomplished, he considers himself "the luckiest man on the face of the earth." He accepts the laws of nature as willingly as he accepts the law of society.

Conclusion

In *Pride of the Yankees,* there are similarities with the first film period pertaining to the value of youth, but distinct differences regarding the value tendencies associated with society/women and law/politics. Taking all three sets of values into account leads to the conclusion that the civilized hero tendencies are dominant in the 1942-43 film era.

While it is true that youth is very much the theme of this film era, especially in light of Lou and Eleanor's relationship, it is also true that the youthful images and youthful behaviors are always accompanied by images of responsible adulthood and the consequences that result with foolish, youthful behavior. Even Eleanor and Lou's honeymoon comes to an end, and they must deal with its end like adults. Youth is valued in this era, but it does not seem to be an untamed and irresponsible youth like that of the first baseball film period. This is no doubt symbolic of the young going off to fight a war that would cause them to age beyond their years.

It seems clear that the most significant changes occurring from the first period to the second concern the images of women and society. In reality, Lou Gehrig was very hesitant about taking Eleanor for his wife. In fact, some sources say that Lou was quite attached to his mother and unwilling to leave her side (Sobol 1974, 213). Certainly the film shows some of this side of Lou, but Lou is not at all portrayed in the film as one who is uncertain about marrying Eleanor. In the film, Lou and Eleanor fully embrace their marriage and by doing so, embrace the values of the civilized hero.

Moreover, Lou's entire life in the film is the model of the civilized man. He honors his family, his country, his job, and his team which undoubtedly is symbolic of the United States. Sam tells us Lou is the best kind of hero there is. He keeps his nose clean, does his job, and does not rock the boat. He is the embodiment of the blue-collar worker.

Women's roles became more noticeably traditional in this second film era. Women are the strong base on which the society is built. They are seen as wholesome, loyal, and supportive. They never complain. This image is emphasized throughout *Pride of the Yankees* as Eleanor continues, in scene after scene, to commemorate Lou's accomplishments by building his scrapbook. There are no words spoken in these scenes. While music of "I'll Be Loving You Always" plays, several shots of Eleanor working in the scrapbook and newspaper articles are superimposed together, an indication of her undying dedication. The images of women in this period seem consistent with the images of the idealized woman that American servicemen overseas probably had during this war era. Perhaps the loyal, supportive women were the kinds of women they hoped would be back in the states waiting for their return.

Pride of the Yankees was released in June of 1942. Lou Gehrig died in June of 1941. The Yankees won the World Series in 1941, and, of course, just two months later, the Japanese bombed Pearl Harbor sending the United States into World War II. These facts are obviously significant to the history of this film period. *Pride of the Yankees* reflects the mood and tenor of the American people just moving out of a period of isolationism and economic and psychological depression into a worldwide conflict. It was certainly representative of the full-blown cooperative spirit that inspired our nation during the troubled years of the war. *Pride of the Yankees* supplies some of the necessities Garth Jowett asserts were required during this historical period:

> The Depression as we have seen, precipitated a reevaluation of the basis of American life, and this mood was carried over into the war years, but with a more precise purpose. In a world convulsed by new ideologies and false issues it was necessary to reaffirm a faith in Democracy, only now it needed more than ever before to be imbued with positive virtues and with a virile and aggressive mass spirit (Jowett 1976, 313).

Pride of the Yankees served this purpose.

Notes

1. Included in the list of Academy Award nominations were Best Picture,

Best Actor, Best Actress, Best Original Story, and Best Cinematography (Nash and Ross 1986, 2454). It is interesting to note that Gary Cooper had starred in another biography, *Sergeant York* (1941), just one year before *Pride of the Yankees* for which he won the Oscar for Best Actor. He had also been nominated for best actor in 1936 for his role in *Mr. Deeds Goes to Town*. In addition to being nominated for best actress in *Pride of the Yankees*, Teresa Wright won the Best Supporting Actress Academy Award for her role in another 1942 production, *Mrs. Miniver* (*The New York Times, Directory of the Film* 1971, 8). Of the four baseball films in this era, only *Pride of the Yankees* and *Ladies' Day* were viewed for this research.

2. Frawley appears in seven of the forty-one films covered in this study.

3. However, it is unreasonable to conclude that the amount of popularity associated with a given team will always be an accurate predictor of what cities' teams appear in the baseball films in any given era. If this were true, then all of the films in the first film era would have been about the New York Yankees, given the immense popularity of the Babe and the tremendous success of the Yankees during that era.

4. The need for a qualifier here is justified by the fact that *Ladies' Day*, the only other film viewed in this period, features a scene where four of the teammates' wives abduct the star pitcher's wife and keep her in an apartment against her will until the World Series is over so that the pitcher can concentrate on winning the World Series. Given the historical context of this film period, the "going outside the law theme" does not seem to fit into the value system of the time.

Biographies and the Forces of Good and Evil (1948-1958)

T he bombing of Hiroshima and Nagasaki, marking the end of World War II for the United States, occurred almost three years prior to the beginning of the third baseball film era.

The end of World War II caused two significant events to occur that would impact on the culture of the fifties. One of these events was the cooling off of diplomatic relations between the United States and the Soviet Union that would eventually develop into the "Cold War," a war that lasted well into the sixties. Secondly, the end of World War II brought the issue of civil rights into the open in America.

The Cold War, fought with political ideologies rather than guns and bombs, created a great deal of suspicion and distrust for communism and communist sympathizers in the United States. The worry and fear of communism that captivated the minds of many Americans, rose to extreme levels and, according to Alonzo Hamby, "created a climate of anticommunist hysteria" (Hamby 1976, 153).

In the late 1940s several accusations of communist-backed espionage were leveled against several United States government officials. This served to trigger an historical period generally known as the "Red Scare." In this period, that lasted beyond the death of one of the most heralded anticommunists of the era, Senator Joseph McCarthy, mainstream America commonly suspected intellectuals and liberals, in all walks of life, as potential communists, since liberals and intellectuals tended to align themselves with the socialistic policies of the FDR administration and tended to be, in the main, open to various political ideologies (Hofstadter 1963, 12). Actress Myrna Loy recalls how she became a suspected communist:

> All you had to do was know someone of questionable political persuasion and you were labeled "Commie.". . . I was one of the first

58

they went for in 1946. If you were a staunch Democrat, politically
involved, and a friend of Eleanor Roosevelt, if you advocated
peace in the United Nations, you were ripe for picking. . . . Most of
us were just good liberals. . . . Hollywood right-wingers feared any
kind of intellectualism (Kotsilibas-Davis 1987, 24-25).

Moreover, according to Caughey and May, the majority of the population at the time "approved of extra legal persecution of communists and
agreed that the hunt for communist influence should take precedence over the
preservation of traditional civil liberties" (Caughey and May 1964, 679). The
Korean War that pitted the communist-supported North Koreans against the
American-supported South Koreans underscored the issue of communism
versus democracy.

The Cold War, the Korean War, the Red Scare, and McCarthyism,
all helped to create a fifties decade some historians refer to as the anti-
intellectual decade, a decade that was characterized by conservative politics,
business supremacy, and a low regard for education. The convincing victory
of General Dwight D. Eisenhower over the highly intellectual Democrat Ad-
lai Stevenson was prophetic of the politically conservative years that lay
ahead.

According to historian Richard Hofstadter, after twenty years of
Democratic rule,

During which the intellectual had been in the main understood
and respected, business had come back into power. . . . Now the
intellectual, dismissed as an "egghead," an oddity, would be gov-
erned by a party which had little use for or understanding of him,
and would be made the scapegoat for everything from the income
tax to the attack on Pearl Harbor (Hofstadter 1963, 4).

The second significant event directly related to World War II was
the increased attention given to the civil rights of blacks in the United States.
Although segregated from whites, black soldiers had fought for the same
freedoms in World War II that the whites had fought for. At the conclusion of
the war, several civil rights activists used the war to argue that all blacks
should be given the rights they were entitled to as United States citizens. Although there were other intervening variables, e.g., economic, the war situation provided a great deal of publicity for the social plight of blacks.

The United States war propaganda brought America's race problems
into sharp focus. The United States' war message stressed above all else the
abhorrence of Hitler's racial bigotry and his bogus theories about racial supremacy. Increasingly, whites had to confront the hypocrisy of their domestic

practices in relationship to their war aims (Bruce 1985, 107).

Black leaders finally began to have their demands for racial equality heard by government officials. Roosevelt had actually started some civil rights legislation while he was in office, but it was Truman who placed federal support for minority groups at the top of his presidential agenda. Truman proposed a fair employment practices act for minorities, a statute to make lynching a federal crime, and another statute that would attempt to end racial discrimination in housing and public transportation (Caughey and May 1964, 660). According to Alonzo Hamby,

> Truman, became the first President since reconstruction to advocate civil rights legislation designed specifically to assist the Black quest for first-class citizenship (Hamby 1976, 149).

Perhaps these initial steps of the civil rights movement did not significantly and directly affect the content of baseball films in this era (although the "Steppin Fetchit" stereotype that frequently appeared in the early Warner Bros. and World War II era films diminished, and *The Jackie Robinson Story* was released during this era), but indirectly, the movement did add to the uneasiness many people already felt during this period due to the threat of communism. Certainly, the blacks and intellectuals (actually, both were symbolic of anti-status quo dissidents) of the era were perceived as obstacles in the path of America's attempt to establish a status quo that reflected capitalism and "business as usual." It would be two more decades before blacks were to see significant changes in their civil rights. But Truman's proposals at least lent some official support to the black cause. Without the nation's attention tuned to civil rights, it may have been several more years before Jackie Robinson or some other black broke the color barrier into professional baseball. In October of 1945, Jackie Robinson signed a major league contract to play with the Brooklyn Dodgers' minor league team in Montreal.

Generally, it seems as though the fifties were representative of a time when this nation, one that had in previous eras welcomed pluralistic values, saw pluralism as a negative concept. According to Henry Kariel, pluralism, which he indicates is "individual freedom," was destroyed in the period due to the tremendous push of our institutions toward sameness for the good of society (Kariel 1965, 179-187). The baseball films of the post-World War II period reflected these attitudes and changes.

This film period produced the greatest number of baseball films (seventeen) and lasted longer than any other baseball film era.[1] All but four of the seventeen films released in this period fit into one of two categories that I have constructed and labeled biography and *Deus Ex Machina* films.

The first category of films, biographies, should be self-explanatory.

There are six films in this category: *The Babe Ruth Story* (1948), *The Stratton Story* (1949), *The Jackie Robinson Story* (1950), *Pride of St. Louis* (1952), *The Winning Team* (1952) and *Fear Strikes Out* (1957). These films are further characterized by the commonality that all are about baseball players who had to endure and overcome some unusual hardship on their way to success, e.g., abandonment, amputation, racial discrimination, a sore arm, alcoholism, and mental illness.

The parameters of the second category of films are not as clearly marked as the biography category but clearly do share a common characteristic. All seven films that fall into this group called *Deus Ex Machina* have some sort of improbable device introduced as a means for resolving the difficulties of the plot. For example, *It Happens Every Spring* (1949) features a liquid chemical substance that repels wood. A college chemistry professor becomes a pitching star by rubbing a baseball with the substance prior to delivering each pitch. Two films, *Kid from Cleveland* and *Kid from Left Field* (1953), have children as the sources of special youthful powers that inspire their teams to win. *Rhubarb* (1951) features a cat that must be present at each game in order to bring an absolutely inept team the power and ability to win. *Angels in the Outfield* (1951) features invisible angels as suppliers of the winning edge, and *Damn Yankees* (1958) features a characterization of Lucifer himself as the winning force. Finally, there is *Roogie's Bump* in which a ghost helps a youngster become the youngest player ever to play major league baseball.

The remaining four films, *Take Me Out to the Ball Game* (1949), *Kill the Umpire*, *Big Leaguer* (1953), and *Great American Pastime*, do not seem to fit with the other thirteen of this period. *Take Me Out to the Ball Game* has already been mentioned in the second chapter as being a remake of the earlier musical *They Learned About Women* (1930), and it certainly seems much more like the films of the first film era than the third. *Kill the Umpire* is a bit like *Big Leaguer* in that the former provides insights into what it takes to be a baseball umpire and the latter portrays the life of a young man trying to crack the big leagues. However, *Kill the Umpire* is more of a humorous entertainment piece while *Big Leaguer* is more of a serious docudrama type of film. *Great American Pastime*, the last of the four atypical films of this period, is, according to Zucker and Babich, the forerunner of *The Bad News Bears* (1976) without the cursing (Zucker and Babich 1987, 21).[2]

The number of baseball films produced in this era represents the most prolific era for the production of baseball films. The seventeen baseball pictures released in this ten-year period represents six more than had been released in the twenty-year span preceding this era and almost double the number of baseball films released in the twenty-seven years that follow this period. It is important to attempt to provide some possible explanations for this curiosity.

Comparing the number of baseball films to the total number of films produced in the same ten-year span, 1948-1958, shows a negative correlation between the number of U.S.-produced films and the number of baseball films produced. The number of films produced in the United States actually declined noticeably in the same ten-year period. For example, in 1948 there were 366 American-made films released, in 1958 there were just 241, and five years later the number dropped to 121. The year 1957 marked the first year that the United States imported more films than it produced (Steinberg 1980, 42).

If there were fewer films produced in Hollywood, it seems logical that the films that did get made were films that came from previously successful formulas and genres. However, this does not appear to be a valid assumption to make about the baseball films of this period. *The Pride of the Yankees* was an above-average box office success in the previous era, having grossed just under $4,000,000 (1942 dollars). But in the fifties-era films, *The Stratton Story* tops the list of baseball film gross revenue earners with $3,700,000. However, six of the seventeen and five out of the last six films released in this period earned less than $1,000,000. The average gross income for the baseball films of this period was around $1,650,000. It does not seem logical to think that Hollywood produced these films with the expectation that they would be tremendously successful, based on their previous earnings (figures compiled from first or second week of January issues of *Variety* from 1942 to 1958).

According to the baseball attendance figures taken from the *Ronald Encyclopedia of Baseball* (1962), major league attendance peaked in 1949 to twenty-one million, but then steadily declined to fourteen million in 1953, then gradually climbed back up to nearly seventeen and one-half million in 1958. Based on major league attendance figures, there seems to be no significant correlation between the popularity of baseball and the number of baseball films produced with the exception that 1949 was the peak of major league attendance and the year Hollywood released four baseball films. Certainly Hollywood had no means of predicting that baseball attendance would increase in 1949.

Another possible explanation for the quantity of baseball films produced in this era relates to the growing popularity of televised baseball. The very first major league game to be televised was between the Cincinnati Reds and the Brooklyn Dodgers on August 26, 1939. After that event, televised baseball continued to gain popularity through 1951, when for the first time, the World Series was available to the national viewing audience (Smith 1987, 45). Television's viewing audience increased 4,000 percent from 1947 to 1948 and the number of licensed television stations in the nation increased from a little over 100 during the freeze period (1948-1952) to 400 stations in

1952, when the license freeze was lifted. The number of television sets sold "increased 500 percent over the 1947 level and by 1951 had already surpassed radio set sales" (Head and Sterling 1982, 187). Television undoubtedly had a significant impact on the film medium, and the film industry had to make some adjustments to combat the popularity of television. According to Jowett,

> The years between 1948 and 1957 were possibly the most important years in the history of the motion picture industry, for it was during this period that the full impact of television was felt, and in the end it was the movies which had to make the adjustment to the acknowledged supremacy of the newer medium (Jowett 1976, 353).

Perhaps the number of baseball films in this period is reflective of Hollywood's attempts to capitalize on the popularity of televised baseball which had grown steadily. By 1954, the Milwaukee Braves remained the only major league baseball team that prohibited the televising of any of their games (*Time*, April 26, 1954, 104).

The answer to the question "Why did Hollywood produce so many baseball films in the fifties?" is probably due to a combination of any of the aforementioned possibilities. Perhaps baseball contained the essence of a value system that needed to be reinforced during this chaotic period. Perhaps veiled within America's national pastime, Hollywood was able to express the true mood and tenor of the television era.

The Films

In order to facilitate the discussion of the films of this period, a representative film has been chosen from each of the two film categories, biography and *Deus Ex Machina*, for the primary focus of the discussion offered here.

The most popular film of this era, judging by box office receipts, was *The Stratton Story* (1949) which had gross revenues close to $4,000,000 (*Variety* 1950, 59). It was produced by MGM and starred James Stewart, June Allyson, and Agnes Moorehead. It was directed by Sam Wood, the director of *Pride of the Yankees*. The popular acclaim and appeal of James Stewart probably had a lot to do with the film becoming "a smash hit that touched the hearts of the country" (Nash and Ross 1986, 3170). Stewart had already won an Academy Award for best actor for his role in *The Philadelphia Story* (1940), and Academy Award nominations for Best Actor for *Mr. Smith Goes to Washington* (1939) and *It's a Wonderful Life* (1946). He had what Janet Lorenz called a "laconic style and boyish manner that seemed to be the embodiment of uncomplicated honesty" (Vinson 1986, 591). Allyson, dubbed by critic Bill Wine as the "quintessentially sweet woman," was the image of wholesomeness and the prototypical devoted-and-steadfast wife of the 1950s (Vinson 1986, 11).

This film is chosen as the representative biography due to the marked popularity of the film and its cast and due also to the judgment that this was one of the higher quality and more believable baseball biographies produced in this period (Nash and Ross 1986, 3170).

The film of choice as the representative film of the *Deus Ex Machina* category is the moderately popular *It Happens Every Spring*, also a 1949 film. This film's gross revenues were almost exactly half that of *The Stratton Story* (*Variety* 1950, 59). The main acting attraction in the film was Ray Milland, who won the Academy Award for Best Actor in 1945 for his role in *The Lost Weekend* (Vinson 1986, 435). The only other film in this category that was more successful in this period was *Damn Yankees* (1958). It does not seem appropriate to select *Damn Yankees* as representative of the era even though it was more financially successful than *It Happens Every Spring*, since it came at the end of the era and also because its main appeal was probably as a musical. The films selected as representative films, *The Stratton Story* and *It Happens Every Spring*, provide some consistency because of their release times.

In addition, they both were relatively successful films, and they both were evaluated by contemporary critics as quality representations of baseball authenticity. In reference to *It Happens Every Spring*, Nash and Ross state, "the baseball footage itself is a marvel as Director Bacon manages to reproduce an atmosphere that appears completely authentic" (Nash and Ross 1986, 1423).

The Stratton Story begins with the hero, Monty Stratton, pitching in a local semi-pro league and being discovered by a scout. The scout (Frank Morgan) offers to help Monty (James Stewart) into the major leagues as they walk back to an isolated farm house in rural Texas where Monty lives with his mother (Agnes Moorehead). Against his mother's preferences, Monty works hard to make the major leagues. Barney (Morgan) convinces Mother Stratton to let him take Monty to Los Angeles for a tryout with the Chicago White Sox who are in spring training there.

Monty gets his tryout and while he is in training, he meets Ethel (June Allyson) and they fall in love. They want to get married, but Monty will not ask Ethel until he has made the White Sox major league team. He finally makes the team, they get married, and they seem extremely happy. They appear to be cut from the same mold as Eleanor and Lou Gehrig, with one major difference. Ethel and Monty have a baby.

Frank Morgan, James Stewart, The Stratton Story *(1949). Photo courtesy of the Museum of Modern Art Film Archives, N.Y.*

Monty returns to his mother's home to join Ethel and the baby after his second full successful season with the White Sox. He inadvertently shoots himself in the leg while on a solo hunting trip and must have his leg amputated in order to live. He struggles through painful interpersonal relationships and psychologically battles a prosthetic leg until his young toddler son, who is just learning to walk, inspires him to learn how to walk on the prosthesis.

Since all Monty ever wanted to do was play baseball, he is encouraged by Ethel, and his own perserverance, drive, and work ethic to try and pitch again. He eventually plays in an area semi-pro all-star game, learns to effectively deal with his handicap, and his team wins the game. Although he never makes it back to the major leagues, an omniscient sounding voice tells the audience at the end of the film,

> Monty Stratton has not won just a ballgame. He's won a greater victory as he goes on pitching, winning, and leading a rich full life. He stands as an inspiration to all of us. He's living proof of what a man can do if he has the courage and determination to refuse to admit defeat.

The same words could have followed any of the biography films. Through courage and determination, Babe Ruth overcame his parental abandonment, Grover Cleveland Alexander overcame alcoholism, and Jackie Robinson overcame the racial barriers, and so on. At the conclusion of the *Jackie Robinson Story* the narrator's voice speaks similar words to those spoken in *The Stratton Story.*

> This is not Jackie Robinson's victory alone. It is a story, a victory that can only happen in a country that is truly free, a country where every child has the opportunity to be the President or play baseball for the Brooklyn Dodgers (*The Jackie Robinson Story*).

The messages are almost identical. In a country that is free and democratic, men and women can, by hard work and determination, become whatever they want to become. This is very similar to the tone and message the audiences were given in *Pride of the Yankees* in 1942. The biographies are essentially serious and dramatic.

On the other hand, the *Deus Ex Machina* films are all on the lighter side. Ghosts, spirits, and good luck charms are not an area of our culture that are normally regarded as serious or realistic. In order to deal with the absurdity of these external forces, the audiences must be able to laugh outwardly. However, there are some serious messages communicated in the subtexts of these comedies.

The earliest and one of the most popular of this film type is *It Happens Every Spring*. Vernon Simpson (Ray Milland) is a college chemistry professor who, as the college President, Dr. Greenleaf (Ray Collins), says, "Should have earned his Ph.D. years ago." The reason Vernon hasn't earned his Ph.D. is because he becomes irresponsible and out of control when baseball season rolls around.

Vernon has been dating Debbie Greenleaf (Jean Peters), daughter of the college president, for quite some time but he will not marry her until he perfects an experiment that he is close to mastering. The formula that he is working on is a bug repellant for trees. He and Debbie are in his lab talking when someone hits a baseball through his lab window and breaks the container holding the liquid repellant. The liquid inadvertently spills on the baseball. Subsequently, Vernon discovers that the formula-coated baseball repels wood.

After hearing on the radio that St. Louis needs pitchers, Vernon goes there to try to help them win the pennant, without telling the college officials or Debbie about his discovery or his plans.

Upon his arrival in St. Louis, Vernon is afforded an opportunity to show them that he can strike out even their best hitters. He is signed to a contract and subsequently wins 38 regular season games for the Cardinals and helps them win the World Series. A humorous scene in the film takes place when in the last game of the series, Vernon runs out of the repellant and is forced to pitch the ninth inning without his special formula. He breaks his hand, making the final out of the game, and is told that he will never pitch again. He is relieved when everybody finds out his true identity. Consistent with the Depression era films, after the series is won, Vernon and Debbie get married.

Each of the other films in this category are developed along similar lines. The team is not doing well and is headed for a dismal season when the unlikely external force, e.g., a kid, a cat, an angel, the devil, or a ghost, enters the picture and the destiny of the team is altered and they eventually win the World Series or the League Championship in the ninth inning of the last game.

Youth and Aging

In the case of the biography baseball films, the fifties was a period when the producers made the value of youth increasingly explicit. *The Babe Ruth Story* opens with a series of shots of young boys wandering around the Baseball Hall of Fame at Cooperstown admiring all the memorabilia. The Babe's dying words are, "people should always be like kids. . . . They've been with me when I was up and when I was down." The narrator at the end of the film assures the audience that Babe Ruth's "name will live as long as there's a ball, a bat, and a boy."

The Jackie Robinson Story also opens with a sequence of shots showing little boys playing baseball, and, as already indicated, it ends by lecturing the audience about a country being truly free when a child can become president or a Brooklyn Dodger. The entire story of Dizzy Dean, in *The Pride of St. Louis*, is a "Peter Pan" like story. Dean basically refuses to grow up even after an injury forces him out of baseball. The heart of the film illustrates how difficult it is for Dizzy to adjust to the realities of adulthood after his baseball playing days have ended.

The critical aspect of the biography films of this period is that they are all about baseball heroes who have to overcome tremendous handicaps and hardships on their way to success and adulthood. The hardships serve to demark the abrupt ending of their youth and the beginning of a new, more mature life. It may be argued here that *The Babe Ruth Story* is about one of the most renowned baseball players ever to play the game, and his story would probably have been made on film regardless of the difficult childhood he experienced. Similarly, *The Jackie Robinson Story* is about the first black ever to play major league baseball, so it, too, perhaps stands alone. However, the same cannot be said about the other biographies. They are about players whose skills ranged from average to good during their careers. The significance of their stories is not only in the quality of their playing, but more importantly, the unusual hardships they endure. Such is the case of *The Stratton Story*.

Monty Stratton is much like Lou Gehrig in that both had an intense, burning desire to play baseball. Each was close to his hardworking mother who did not approve of her son playing baseball because of the game's association with foolishness and child's play.

Monty, after pitching nine innings of baseball and running home ten miles to his farm, is chastised by his mother for playing ball . . . again. "That's a fine way for the man of the family to be spending his time," Mother Stratton scolds (Monty's father died and left the farm to him). Monty wants to play ball and please his mother at the same time, so he gets up early and does his chores, earns $3 pitching in a game in which he makes such quick order of the other team that he still has time "to pick a little cotton, if he runs home." The scene is symbolic of the endless pools of energy and enthusiasm associated with youthful desire and drive.

Barney (Frank Morgan), the former baseball player and would-be scout, follows Monty home after seeing him pitch and tells Mrs. Stratton, "I'd say he's got a great future in baseball." Mrs. Stratton sees the shabby attire of Barney, who looks like he has been homeless for a while, and asks, "You a baseball man?" "Yes Maam," he responds. "I'd say he's got a better future on the farm," she snaps. Barney and Monty scheme together, like two young brothers trying to have their way with a parent, so that Barney can stay and prepare Monty for a major league baseball career.

Later Monty is signed by the White Sox. He has yet to get paid, and so he has very little money. Needing a haircut, he goes to the barbershop with just enough money to pay for his haircut. While he is waiting for his turn, he sees some men gambling on "one-armed bandits" and decides to give it a try himself. He begins to drop all of his haircut money into the machine without any thought that he will not be able to get his haircut if he has no money. He is down to his last quarter when he hits the jackpot. Like a child, he seems to be oblivious to the risks he takes, e.g., going to Los Angeles on a whim and losing his money on gambling.

Emotionally, Monty seems to let external forces dictate his moods. When things are going well, he is optimistic, energetic, and fun-loving. After the amputation, he sulks, pouts, and rejects family companionship and general attempts by his loved ones to soothe his wounds, much like a little boy would act upon encountering a difficult situation. Some degree of hostility after such a tragedy is understandable, but Monty's illogical and irrational behavior seems adolescent and immature. The more Ethel and Mother Stratton attempt to console and comfort him, the more unreasonable his behavior becomes.

However, for the most part, Monty displays an adult awareness of his responsibilities before and after he makes the White Sox. He does his chores on the farm, he feels guilty about getting paid to sit on the White Sox bench while he is breaking in, and he defends the honor of a fellow rookie's girlfriend when it becomes obvious that the other rookie is mistreating her and acting rude to her in public.

In general, it appears as though the value of youth as it is portrayed in the biographies of this era is more in line with that of the *Pride of the Yankees* era rather than the Joe E. Brown baseball film period. The biography films are symbolic of a childhood lost or cut short by the circumstances faced. Typically, the heroes are forced to grow up early. This is especially the case with Babe Ruth in *The Babe Ruth Story* and Jimmy Piersall in *Fear Strikes Out*. Many of Piersall's psychological problems seem directly related to the fact that his father prohibited him from having a childhood and from displaying childish emotions and behaviors that other children display.

Formal education is typically not an issue in these films as it was in the previous periods. Other than Jackie Robinson and his brother attending college and Dizzy Dean talking about his lack of education, the topic is not even mentioned. In the two films where education is discussed, it is not held in very high regard. Robinson only goes to college so that he has more opportunities to play sports. Due to his color, a college education will not necessarily guarantee him any kind of success. (His brother earned a four-year college degree, and the best job he could get was a street sweeper.)

Dizzy Dean's lack of education adds to his folksy appeal and, eventually, to his popularity as a baseball broadcaster. He was notorious for "butchering" the English language. The concerned teachers and education administrators of St. Louis, who complained about the harm Dizzy was doing to the young boys of America, are portrayed as being heartless, insensitive, un-American, and unjustified in their accusations and concern for Dizzy's lack of proper grammar. Clearly, education is not a top priority.

Judging from the above data, it would appear as though Hollywood created two conflicting messages regarding youth and aging in this period. Explicitly, the audience is told that baseball, the national game, is representative of the youthful spirit of America. At the same time, the films imply that the baseball heroes in these films have had to circumvent their youthful ways and desires in order to become successful baseball heroes. The dialogue of Dizzy Dean's wife in *Pride of St. Louis* lends further support to this contention. As she prepares to leave him and thereby end their relationship she says, "You're a child. . . . It just isn't possible to be a child all of your life." Dean is forced to grow up, if he wants to be accepted by the other adults of society. Even though the Babe advises that "everyone should be like kids," the reality in the fifties was that baseball was played by adults in an adult world, and those who succeeded and became heroes were adults, not children.

The *Deus Ex Machina* films have several similarities with the biography films of this era regarding the value of youth and aging. In *It Happens Every Spring*, Vernon Simpson is the stereotypical egghead professor who has youthful desires to play baseball. When the opportunity to play professional baseball presents itself, he drops all of his collegiate responsibilities and travels off to fulfill his dream. Rather than tell his peers, colleagues, and girlfriend where he is going or what he is doing, Vernon just asks them to trust and understand him.

Vernon's boss, the Chairman of the Chemistry Department, thinks Vernon is one of the finest researchers and chemistry scholars around, yet he acknowledges that Vernon seems to be out of control every spring. He seems to believe that Vernon's spring-time problems are related to basic biological desires. As he states to President Greenleaf:

> From October to April Vernon's alert, conscientious, and an excellent teacher, but every spring he seems to undergo a peculiar change. He becomes absentminded to a degree. It's like spring fever (*It Happens Every Spring*).

These images of Vernon are symbolic of the biological changes that take place in younger men during adolescence and represent an appeal that emphasizes the glory of youth and nature. Vernon cannot resist giving in to his adolescent desires.

The transformation that occurs in the spring for Vernon is really caused by his infatuation with baseball, as is demonstrated by his toting a radio into his chemistry class and listening to it while he is lecturing. His attention is easily turned away from his classroom duties to the broadcast of a baseball game.

Beyond the above examples, there are few references to youth in this film. Most of the time Vernon reflects behavior that is more typical of an intellectual adult than of an irrational and emotional child. However, at times his intellectualism results in misunderstanding when he explains his situation and point of view from various levels of abstraction. For example, he attempts to explain to Debbie Greenleaf (Jean Peters), his girlfriend, how he feels about her. He is unable to do so in a clear fashion due to all of the qualifiers he adds to his explanation of his feelings. Unlike the Joe E. Brown characters of the earlier period, Vernon's problem is not that he is unable to find the words to say, but rather, he has so many words at his disposal that they only serve to confuse the receiver.

Debbie: ... You're so terribly vague ...
Vernon: I'm very definite about you, why you're almost every-

	thing I ever think about-*almost*. What else can I say?
Debbie:	Something concrete, something positive.
Vernon:	Oh, but it's been out of the question until now . . . I'm serious, Debbie. That's why I can't say anything because if a man is serious, he doesn't have the right to say anything until he can be serious. . . . I'm talking about three hours from now, maybe sooner, maybe any minute, in less than three minutes, I will know about my experiment.

In a similar sequence, later in the film, Vernon tries to explain to his roommate, Lanigan (Paul Douglas), about his predicament when Lanigan asks about Vernon's picture of Debbie.

Vernon:	Well, it's her father. If he ever finds out, I'll lose my girl, my job, and everything.
Lanigan:	Finds out what?
Vernon:	What I'm doing. I didn't think I could do it but I am. What I'm doing isn't what he thinks I'm doing at all.
Lanigan:	Come again.
Vernon:	Well, I'm getting the one thing he wants me to have by doing the one thing he's most against. You see?
Lanigan:	Leave it go, Kelly. Quit trying. The more you talk, the more mysterious it gets.

These abstract conversations seem to be indicative of the problems that occur as a result of too much education. The educated intellectual is unable to communicate with the uneducated.

The issue of education versus athletic prowess is a deliberate issue in this film. In a very early sequence, President Greenleaf is asked to speak at a football banquet. He declines, saying, "I'm trying to de-emphasize athletics, not glorify them." Vernon is very much aware of President Greenleaf's disapproval of sports and games, which explains Vernon's previous speech to Lanigan. President Greenleaf finds his daughter Debbie reading the sports page after Vernon confesses his alternate identity and says to Debbie, "You're not becoming a sports fan are you?," as though a sports fan is the worst thing a scholar could waste his/her time on.

However, it is the athlete who wins out over the intellectual because the owner of the St. Louis Cardinals, upon winning the World Series, presents President Greenleaf with a large endowment for his college's chemistry department. Winning the World Series was made possible by Vernon's repellant discovery and its application in athletics.

Other films in this category have implications similar to the biographies regarding the value of youth. Even though in *Kid from Left Field*, a young boy provides the motivation and impetus for the team to rally, regroup, and win the pennant, the boy is actually more of an adult than he is a child. Chris (Billy Chapin) does not play baseball like the rest of the boys his age; he manages a major league baseball team. Even when he is with his friends, he manages their little league team. He does not play. Chris has no mother. His father, Larry Cooper (Dan Dailey), a former minor league caliber player, is irresponsible, childlike, and sulks about not being able to play baseball. Chris takes care of his father and their finances. Again, this is a story of an abbreviated childhood.

Summary of Value of Youth and Aging

With few exceptions, the value of youth in this period is very similar to that of the last period. Even though the films, in some cases, give unequivocal cues that say youth is valuable and is a positive trait, there seems to be little doubt that the dominant tendency with regard to youth in this period is that mature and responsible behavior, typically associated with the aging process, is more appropriate than is the behavior of the irrational child. The message to the audience from these films is "grow up, be responsible, and be realistic."

At the same time there tends to be an anti-intellectual or anti-education message in the films of this period which is very different from the message of the *Pride of the Yankees* era. Education seems to be attached to behavior that is irresponsible and unrealistic in the baseball films of the fifties. Education is for children. The films seem to say that it is unnecessary for adults to be educated unless education leads them to better employment. Lou Gehrig's mother realized the number of opportunities that would be afforded an educated person in America in the 1942-43 era. But in the 1948-1958 period there are no pro-education messages present. Professor Greenleaf makes an issue out of emphasizing academics over athletics in *It Happens Every Spring,* but he ultimately loses his battle when Vernon shows that his athletic ability leads him to financial independence and his formal education and teaching career did not.

The value of aging and anti-intellectualism/education in the films of this period seems to be consistent with the dominant attitudes of distrust and fear of the unknown and anti-intellectualism of the cultural milieu of the period. The realities of the military casualties that many suffered after World War II, and during and after the Korean War, probably accounted for some of the tendency of the films to de-glorify youth. Many soldiers had lost their "youth" in the wars. It is also probable that the naiveté, honesty, and openness that frequently typifies youthful behavior were not desirable traits when dealing with the "red menace" that threatened American social and economic stability. To thwart the threat of the menace, which could be anywhere at anytime, an adult's suspicious and cynical eyes would be more appropriate than a child's.

Women and Society

It is interesting to note that out of all the seventeen films in this era, only two, *Take Me Out to the Ball Game* and *Damn Yankees,* have a woman that could be considered a vamp. Interestingly enough, both of these films are musicals and the vamp in both is a singer/dancer. Moreover, in *Damn Yankees*, the vamp, the devil's assistant, is a 172-year-old witch (Gwen Verdon) who looks about 150 years younger than she is. She is the classic model of the woman who tries to prevent the baseball hero from delivering the championship to his team. Ultimately, as in all baseball films, she does not succeed.

The female roles in the biography baseball films of this era are truly exemplary of the traditional American woman and traditional American values established in prior years. As previously stated, each hero in the biographies overcomes personal hardships. It is the wife (every one of the heroes featured in these biography films is married) who lends her support and undying loyalty to the hero as he suffers through his setbacks. The exception to this scenario is Patricia Dean (Joanne Dru) in *Pride of St. Louis.*

After Dizzy Dean is injured in an all-star game and eventually has to quit baseball, he cannot accept the fact that his career is over and refuses to adjust to a new style of life. Pat leaves him because of what she perceives as his refusal to grow up. However, she tells him that it is up to him if and when she comes back. Dizzy gets a job as a radio baseball commentator, adjusts to his new role, and Pat comes back home.

It is significant that June Allyson plays the role of Ethel Stratton in *The Stratton Story* because she is, as Bill Wine said, "the quintessentially sweet woman" of the fifties. The character she portrays is very much like the Eleanor Gehrig character in *Pride of the Yankees.*

After Monty's leg is amputated, he interacts with her disrespectfully, if he interacts with her at all. Yet, she never loses her temper, patience, or compassion. She finally nurtures him back on his feet and initiates his road to full recovery by throwing the baseball with him. The point here is that Allyson's character is developed completely around the traditional image of the wholesome, loyal, and supportive woman. At one point in the film, shortly after the accident, Allyson's "mother-earth" image and wholesomeness is underscored when she is seen in bib-overalls, a plaid flannel shirt, and her hair in pigtails a la *Rebecca of Sunnybrook Farm.*

The concept of loyalty and fidelity ties many of these films together. It is characteristic of several films in this period, biographies and *Deus Ex Machina* films alike, that no matter what the husband says or does to the wife, she remains loyal. It is interesting to note that the husband's loyalty to the wife is also apparent in these films. Divorce is not mentioned and infidelity, although suspected by others, is not an option for either spouse.

One example that illustrates this point occurs when Barney suspects Monty of infidelity. Monty has frequent and regular secret engagements which he will not interrupt and which he will not tell anybody about. Barney worries that Monty is being unfaithful and his image will be damaged if he is. Eventually Barney learns that his worries are unfounded when he finds out that Monty has been taking dancing lessons to please Ethel.

Rural or agrarian values, when present in the biographies, seem to be more openly revered than in the first era. This is a significant change from the first film period. In the first period, the natural hero, who came from the country, was the target of jokes, tricks, and ribbing. There is little of that in this period. There are several examples to support this contention.

One example of the positive portrayal of agrarian values in this film is the haircut scene. It is as though fate rewards Monty with the jackpot because of his situation, a farm boy out of his element and in need. As he collects his winnings, he turns to the men, who were laughing at him using up his money and who now are in awe, and says to them, "It's a good thing I won, I was down to my last quarter."

Later, Monty gets stuck going on a blind date to cover for a friend, Eddie (Bill Williams), who made the date. The date turns out to be Ethel. Monty's friend is hesitant to ask Monty to cover for him because of the way he looks, but he has no other options because all his other teammates are busy. "Hey, country, is that the only suit you got?" Eddie asks. The camera shows the audience what Ethel is seeing when she meets Monty for the first time. He is tall, gangly, and his clothes do not fit him very well. Upon seeing him, Ethel whispers to her friend, who is Eddie's date, "Oh no." But Ethel soon realizes that Monty is easy to get to know, sensitive, and honest. He turns out to be much more honorable than the well-groomed and good-looking Eddie.

Monty seems to have much more common sense than his country hero predecessors. He interprets Eddie's behavior as manipulative and insensitive when Eddie sticks Monty with the cab fare and then tries to "come on" to Ethel while his own girlfriend looks on. Monty yells at Eddie for his behavior and tells Ethel that he is going to take her home. In the cab, Ethel seems quite put off by Monty's presumptuous behavior.

June Allyson, The Stratton Story (1949). *Photo courtesy of the Museum of Modern Art Film Archives, N.Y.*

Ethel: Did it occur to you that I might have wanted to go on
         somewhere with Eddie?
Monty: Well, what you wanted wasn't so important.
Ethel: Oh it wasn't?
Monty: No, no. What was important was the way Eddie was
         treatin' Dot. He was tryin' to shine up to you and he
         shouldn't have done it in front of her.
Ethel: Or in front of you?
Monty: No, no, no, no. Nah it's not what I mean. Look I'm sorry
         about tonight. . . . You sorta got stuck with me, didn't
         ya?
Ethel: Ah, that's silly.
Monty: No it isn't. I just never had much experience with girls.
Ethel: (Laughs)
Monty: What's so funny?
Ethel: And then you got stuck with the check.

Here Monty shows his sensitivity and his directness. He communicates his thoughts without any of the indecision and nervousness that seemed
to hinder the Joe E. Brown characters in the early period. But like Gehrig, he
has no experience with girls. However, unlike Gehrig and Brown's characters, no one makes fun of him or gets the better of him. He is not naive like
his earlier counterparts.

Even though, as Monty tells us, he has no experience with girls, and
one would also assume, like the heroes before him, he has no experience with
traditional societal roles and norms, he does not think it is appropriate to take
on a wife until he has some stability in his life. To Monty, that stability is
making it into the big leagues. When he gets sent back to the minors after a
brief period with the parent club, he shares his anxiety with Ethel.

Ethel: Am I your problem? Would it help any if, if I said I love
         you?
Monty: That's the problem.
Ethel: Oh, I see.
Monty: Oh, no, you don't see . . . I . . . no matter what I was
         doin,' I kept thinking about you. Now I don't know
         where I'm going.
Ethel: It doesn't matter to me if you're in the big leagues. . . .
Monty: A man's gotta know where he's goin.'

Ethel does not mind that Monty is in the minor leagues and would
not be able to provide the stability that Monty thinks is necessary for a proper

marriage, but Monty, as the rational, civilized, adult male knows that "a man" must be able to provide for his wife. Monty embraces the traditional, civilized roles of society and knows he must do what is expected of him in order to be a contributing member of that society.

The other heroes in the biographies are very similar to Monty in this respect. Jackie Robinson warns his future wife (Ruby Dee) against marrying him before he has made the Dodgers, "You marry me now and you're asking for trouble." She responds, "O.K. Jackie, I'll ask for it." Team owner, Branch Rickey (Minor Watson), tells Robinson that he is going to need a "girl" to get him through the difficult times that lie ahead of him as the first black in major league baseball. Similarly, Jimmy Piersall (Anthony Perkins), in *Fear Strikes Out,* tries to convince the future Mrs. Piersall (Norma Moore) that she does not want to be tied to a ballplayer's lifestyle of trains, lack of security, and hotels. Almost apologetically he tells her he does not know how to do anything else. In the opening scenes of *The Winning Team,* Grover Cleveland Alexander (Ronald Reagan) is asked by his boss when he is going to get married and Grover's response is, "Soon as I can save up enough for a place of our own . . . I gotta farm all picked out now."

It seems prophetic that in the two biographies where the hero does marry prior to making it to the major leagues, the marriage encounters significant problems. Grover Cleveland Alexander's eventual wife, Aimee (Doris Day), and father-in-law (Frank Ferguson), despise baseball and do everything they can to keep Grover out of it. After he develops diplopia, he promises to settle down and not waste his time playing baseball. But he broods, pouts, and is generally inconsolable. Their marriage seems to be on the rocks. Aimee cries to Grover's mother about how Grover has tried hard to be a farmer, but his first love has always been baseball, and about how she feels unable to compete with baseball for his love. Grover's diplopia eventually goes away, and Aimee agrees that Grover should play professional baseball. She also decides to go with him to spring training. Their marriage is subsequently revitalized.

Similarly, in *Fear Strikes Out,* Jimmy and Mary Piersall's relationship begins very unsteadily as they are married prior to Jimmy's promotion into the big leagues. Even after Jimmy does make it to the majors, their relationship does not proceed well until Jimmy resolves his deep-seated psychological problems. It is reasonable to conclude that the premature marriage may have added to the psychological pressures that Piersall faced.

In all of the instances cited above, it should be clear that the message of the films is that the accepted role for the hero in the civilized society is related to the Andrew Carnegie mind-set referred to earlier in this work, namely, a young man should first succeed and then he will receive the best of all possible rewards, a wife. Make no mistake the wife should come after success, not before.

It is clear in these biography films that the heroes are very much a part of the civilized hero tendency regarding women and society. These heroes do not even recognize that there is an alternative to being married and becoming a part of the status quo. There is no tendency to avoid women or society. It is just a matter of time before the hero becomes married and joins the civilized society.

By comparison, the *Deus Ex Machina* films are not as consistent in their depiction of traditional women's roles and values. For example, in *It Happens Every Spring*, Vernon is hesitant to marry Debbie because of his lack of success and fears that he would be incapable of adequately providing for her. Similarly, Joe Hardy (Tab Hunter), in *Damn Yankees*, breaks a deal with the devil so that he can return to his wife after he has helped the team beat the Yankees in the World Series. These two films seem to contain examples of traditional values, yet the other five films of this category do not explicitly reflect similar traditional tendencies.

With the exception of Joe Hardy, none of the protagonists are married during the films, although the topic of marriage is mentioned with some regularity in all of them. A relevant example occurs in *Rhubarb*. Rhubarb the cat is left an enormous estate under the trusteeship of the Brooklyn Dodgers' Press Agent, Eric Yeager (Ray Milland). Eric must protect Rhubarb from mobsters who want to kill him because of his "good luck" value to the Dodgers. (The mob has money bet against the Dodgers in the World Series.) For Eric, this means keeping the cat close to his side at all times. This, in turn, results in problems for Eric and his fiancée, Polly Sickles (Jan Sterling), because she is allergic to Rhubarb's fur. There are several thwarted attempts by the couple to marry, in spite of the allergy. Finally, after the Dodgers win the pennant, Rhubarb is out of danger, and Polly and Eric are able to get married. It is assumed that Polly and Eric do get married, since one of the last shots of the film is the two of them pushing a baby buggy. But there is no such marriage at the end of *The Kid from Left Field* or *Angels in the Outfield*.

The kid in *The Kid from Left Field* is being raised by his father, and as previously noted, his mother has been dead for sometime. Marian Whacker (Anne Bancroft), is virtually the only woman in the film. She is a career woman who dates Pete Haines (Lloyd Bridges), one of the ballplayers on the team owned by Marian's uncle (Ray Collins). Marian and Pete's marital status is never resolved, and although she supplies some motherly support to the kid, Chris Cooper, she is really not the model of the traditional woman that has been portrayed in practically all baseball films to this point.

Similarly, *Angels in the Outfield* goes against the grain of the traditional role of women. The protagonist in the film is Guffy McGovern (Paul Douglas), the manager of the Pirates. A reporter, Jennifer Paige (Janet Leigh), is assigned to cover the Pirates. It is implied that Guffy and Jennifer begin to fall in love. Their relationship is complicated as both of them become attached to a very cute and precocious orphan girl. Subsequently, the unmarried Guffy considers adopting the little girl without being married. Guffy and Jennifer talk about the adoption. Both realize how difficult it would be for a single parent to adopt the girl, yet neither mentions marriage. The movie ends with the three of them, Guffy, Jennifer, and Brigitte (the little girl) standing at the top of the Pirates stadium, after the Pirates win the pennant, with Guffy saying "Look what I got." The audience assumes he is referring to his new family, but there is no direct evidence to indicate that they do become a family. Even if their relationship is consummated, it certainly does not seem to be representative of traditional roles and values.

As in *Kid from Left Field,* there are no traditional women's roles in this film. Jennifer is a working woman who cannot cook. Her one attempt at being a traditional woman (she prepares a dinner for Guffy and Brigitte that is inedible) fails miserably.

As discussed earlier, children of this era are adult-like. Brigitte is the stabilizing force for Guffy and Jennifer, who seem to remain somewhat immature throughout the film. Both Guffy and Jennifer are hesitant to express any intimate feelings for each other. Young Brigitte is generally very mature, gentle, soft spoken, and optimistic even though she has spent her early years in an orphanage. She seems to have her entire life under control.

There is one additional recurring behavior in two of the films in this era that might be suggestive of a change in contemporary values regarding the traditional husband and wife relationship. In *It Happens Every Spring* and in *Damn Yankees,* the first and last films of this period, there is a characterization that suggests that men have grown tired of their wives. This is not to say that men are depicted as not loving their wives. They do love them and they are faithful and loyal to them, but the men in these films avoid communicating with their wives. Wives are seen, for the first time in baseball films, as pests/ nags or annoyances. This conclusion is based on observations made from a scene in *It Happens Every Spring* and the opening scene of *Damn Yankees.*

In the former, Munk's (Paul Douglas) wife calls the room that Vernon and Munk share to check to see if Munk is cheating on her. Somewhat resentful, Munk assures her that he is not, but she goes on talking anyway. Without hanging up the phone, Munk sets it down while his wife continues to talk. Periodically, Munk stops walking around the room, picks up the phone and says "Yes, Mabel" "Anything you say, Mabel," without listening to what she is saying. Munk then turns to Vernon and asks, "You never been married, have you Kelly?," as Munk shakes his head in disbelief. Even though Munk's marriage does not appear to be a very sensitive, caring, or happy marriage, he does not contemplate being unfaithful to Mabel.

Similarly in *Damn Yankees*, a middle-aged Joe Hardy sits in front of his television set, intensely watching a baseball game. He mumbles vociferously as "his" Senators are losing once again to the Yankees. As he watches the game and mumbles, his wife (Shannon Bolin) sews and talks incessantly about the weather. Neither pays any attention to each other's activity, which prompts her to sing a song about how boring their lives have been and yet they are still content with each other. As Mrs. Hardy announces that she is going to bed, Joe mumbles something about those Damn Yankees and then, thinking better of not acknowledging his wife's announcement, yells up the steps "Good night, ole girl."

Their lives seem rather dull and stale after twenty plus years of marriage, yet there is no desire on the part of either one to break from the boredom until the devil appears on Joe's doorstep and offers him an opportunity to get away from the routine and boredom. Joe hesitates to accept the devil's deal but does accept a contract with an escape clause. In the end, Joe uses the escape clause and eagerly returns to Meg Hardy, more committed to their relationship than ever before. In fact, it is the strength of their renewed relationship which assists Joe in rebuking the devil's last attempts to get him away from Meg. Meanwhile the devil "curses" the institution of marriage.

Summary of Women and Society

Based on the observations discussed above, from both sets of films, it is reasonable to conclude that the films of this period predominantly reinforce the values associated with the civilized hero. Women represent the stabilizing forces of this society. The hero willingly embraces the codes and norms of the society. It is certainly more desirable to be inside the official society than on the outside in these films. The predominant values of the civilized hero's woman are loyalty and stability.

However, the seeds of change of these values are also seen in these films. As indicated previously, for the first time in baseball films, we see the formation of non-traditional families, e.g., Rhubarb is part of Eric and Debbie's family; in *The Kid from Left Field,* Chris Cooper has no mother; *The Kid from Cleveland* is "adopted" by the Cleveland Indians; and Brigitte, the orphan, is being adopted by a single father in *Angels in the Outfield.*

Women's roles begin to show some significant change during this period as well. These changes reflect a condition that actually began during World War II. For example, Eleanor Gehrig was, in reality, a very independent and successful business woman. Her character was not depicted as such in 1942 in *Pride of the Yankees.* However, in the fifties film period there are several main female characters who are career women. The appearance of the career woman in these films seems to be indicative of the increased number of career women who were part of the paid job force during the fifties and is perhaps indicative of a wider acceptance of women out of the traditional family roles,—although the traditional female role for women is back in place with Meg Hardy in the last film of the period, *Damn Yankees*.

Politics and Law

There are really very few cues available in *The Stratton Story* that pertain to politics and the law. Since his rural upbringing has kept him "close" to the land, Monty is quite obviously a character who has generally regarded natural law as being the supreme law. His rural upbringing has consisted mainly of his being familiarized with natural events and laws. His amputation reenforces the strength of the natural laws and emphasized how hopeless man is against natural forces.

The Jackie Robinson Story merits special consideration under politics and the law because this film seems to be, above all else, a statement about how important it is to play by the rules of civilization and society.

Jackie Robinson is depicted as doing all the right things that are supposed to lead to success in America. He works hard shining shoes and delivering papers, he loves his mother, he goes to college, he joins the military, he is true to his family, friends, and country, and yet he fears that he may not be able to get a job because he is black. Just when it looks like Jackie might spend his life playing in the Black Baseball Leagues, he is given an opportunity by the "benevolent" Branch Rickey to play major league baseball.[3]

Rickey asks Robinson to promise that no matter what happens and no matter what anybody says to him, he will not react or retaliate. Here Robinson is being asked to give up any attachments he may have to his natural tendencies. He is asked to abide by a civilized code that is unjust and unfair, but at the same time, it is the code he must embrace completely if he is to be a part of civilization. Robinson wants to be a part of the establishment so much that he agrees to abide by the special rules.

The audience witnesses some of the milder racial slurs thrown his way by the fans, players, and various other bigots. According to Nash and Ross,

> They couldn't really use the language that was thrown at Robinson on the field because that would never have passed the censor. He was the victim of more verbal abuse than any athlete who had ever stepped on a field and he held his normally hot temper in check as a promise to Rickey (Nash and Ross 1986, 1441).

Jackie withstands all of the abuse. It is primarily by the special civilized codes that he succeeds. At the end of the film the words of a speech Jackie gave at the White House are heard:

> I know that life in these United States can be mighty tough for people who are a little different from the majority. I'm not fooled because I've had a chance open to very few Negro Americans, but I do know that democracy works for those who are willing to fight for it and I'm sure it's worth defending. I can't speak for any fifty million people, no one person can but I'm certain that I and other Americans of many races and faiths have too much invested in our country's welfare to throw it away or to let it be taken from us. (*The Jackie Robinson Story*)

With this speech, Jackie has reinforced the principles of democracy. He has committed himself and others to the American dream. Although his speech may be interpreted as a controversial stand for civil rights, in 1950, it is more likely, especially when juxtaposed with shots of the Statue of Liberty, and more accurately interpreted, as a speech in defense of democracy. For it is the civilized laws of a democratic nation that has made his success possible.

In addition to the observations regarding the above-mentioned tendencies in the biographies, three main elements common to several of the films of this period demand some special attention as they pertain to politics and the law. These three elements are: the depiction of gambling, the repetitive presence of trials/courts, and the entire category of what I have labeled *Deus Ex Machina* films.

Elements of illegal gambling are still apparent in the early films of this period but do not appear again after 1951. In each case where gambling is mentioned, it is denounced and sometimes attacked by the hero in the film. For example, a gambler attempts to buy out Babe Ruth in *The Babe Ruth Story* and the Babe hits him in the face. Gamblers try to control the outcome of the "big" game in *Take Me Out to the Ball Game* and Gene Kelly attempts to punch the gambling boss (Edward Arnold) in the face. Finally, in *Rhubarb*, Eric finds out that big time gamblers have stolen Rhubarb so that the Dodgers will lose the game. Eric finds their "hideout," a fight ensues, and Eric forces Pencil Louis (Richard Karlan) to tell him where Rhubarb is and the gambler's crime is prevented.

The heroes in these films are obviously and explicitly against gambling. There is no differentiating between amateur and professional gamblers in the films. Every one of the episodes cited above involves professional gamblers. It is significant that in all three of these films, the gamblers are not apprehended by the appropriate or official authorities. Each incident depicts the hero taking the law into his own hands. This seems to indicate that the law enforcement officials are not as capable of correcting the problem as the heroes are. The films appear to be saying that in some situations the individual must take the law into his or her own hands.

This message could be read as being supportive of the popular attitudes of the fifties that expected private individuals to police communist sympathizers and communist tendencies. Yet the behavior of taking the law "into your own hands" is characteristic of the natural hero and not consistent with the other tendencies of the civilized hero of this period.

Monty Stratton adds a philosophical point of view about gambling that is quite different from the above interpretations. It seems significant that Monty gambled on the one arm bandits at the barbershop as he waited for his haircut. He did not, however, gamble on a baseball game. When Monty shows up for a date with Ethel with his pockets filled with coins that he won from the machines, the following conversation ensues:

Ethel: Well, if you don't make it in baseball you've got a good future in gambling.
Monty: Oh, no, I'm through gambling.
Ethel: Why?
Monty: Well, I've found out what it's like to lose and I've found out what its like to win. . . . Why keep at it?

Monty truly represents the rational, reasonable side of the adult civilized hero.

To date, the repetitive presence of courtrooms and trials is peculiar only to this film era. The situations for which the court proceedings are brought and the fashion in which the proceedings are handled are a bit curious. There are four films, all from the *Deus Ex Machina* category, that contain trials. The four films are *Rhubarb, Angels in the Outfield, The Kid from Left Field,* and *Damn Yankees.*

The trial in *Rhubarb* takes place because the daughter of the team's dead owner is jealous that Eric and Rhubarb were left with basically all of her father's estate. She brings suit against Eric and tries to prove that Rhubarb is dead so that she can receive the estate left to Rhubarb. The plaintiff's attorney brings three identical Rhubarb "look-a-likes" and asks the defendant, Eric, to identify which cat is Rhubarb. The judge asks Eric for conclusive proof of which cat is Rhubarb, and Eric replies "But, I have no conclusive proof, your honor." When the daughter's attorneys push for a settlement, Eric responds, "I'd rather die first. One thing I learned from the old man and this cat, too, is, don't let people push you around. If you're right, fight." Eventually, conclusive proof of Rhubarb's identity is provided by Polly who must sniff each of the cats because the one that makes her sneeze is Rhubarb.

The focus of the trial in *Angels in the Outfield* is on whether or not a manager of a baseball team, Guffy, because he talks to angels, should be deemed psychologically unfit to manage the Pirates' baseball team. What makes this trial so peculiar is that the sports announcer (Keenan Wynn) who brought the charges against Guffy, and who really has no "standing" to bring such charges, is also asking questions at the trial as though he were a prosecuting attorney. Testimony revolves around the appropriateness of the belief in angels. After a psychologist testifies, Guffy calls a professor of religion and philosophy, a rabbi, and a priest to the witness stand. They all support the belief in angels, but the judge/commissioner demands some concrete evidence. Little Brigitte comes in and tells the commissioner everything she saw at the baseball park. Besides Guffy, Brigitte is the only other person who can see the angels. The commissioner is convinced, especially upon seeing a feather fall from the ceiling, that angels exist, and he subsequently drops the case.

Additional courtroom scenes come from Chris Cooper in *Kid from Left Field*, where he is vindicated by a female judge of truancy charges. Joe Hardy's identity is proven by "expert" witnesses in a courtroom scene in *Damn Yankees*, and he also is subsequently freed.

Two significant elements contained in these baseball film trials deserve consideration. First, it is important that the protagonists are vindicated as a result of the court system. Even though the film representations of the American legal system are laughable, nevertheless, in the end, the system is just and reasonable. Again this is very similar to the previous era. This tendency serves to reinforce the civilized hero values.

Second, and probably more important for this era, is the fact that the trials are a symbol of the unreasonable and unjustifiable accusations that some people experienced during the McCarthy era. Charges were lodged against seemingly innocent victims, and allegations were based on very shaky circumstantial evidence, when evidence was presented at all, in several of the McCarthy era proceedings. This explains the judge's desire in *Rhubarb* and *Angels in the Outfield* for some *real* concrete evidence. The filmmakers seemed to be voicing their confidence that McCarthy-like allegations, so prevalent in Hollywood during the "Red Scare," could eventually be resolved through the United States court system and by providing real evidence.

The final element to be discussed in this section pertains to the whole group of *Deus Ex Machina* or supernatural films. There is no other baseball film period that produced these kinds of films, films where ghosts, chemicals, and angels intervene on behalf of someone or some team trying to win the pennant.[4] These films go beyond the natural law tendencies and well beyond the civilized law tendencies. There seems to be no logical explanation for the existence of these supernatural forces. On one hand, the baseball films tell us, through the "normal" hero biographies, that success comes to those

Paul Douglas, Keenan Wynn, Angels in the Outfield *(1951). Photo courtesy of the Museum of Modern Art Film Archives, N.Y.*

who are dedicated, follow the rules, and work hard. On the other hand, these *Deus Ex Machina* films tell us there is no readily available rational way to explain someone's success. How is it that "the gods" smile on a grumpy old man like Guffy and that he wins the pennant? Did he work harder than anyone else? Did he treat his players well? Did he display any of the favorable traits associated with the traditional model of a baseball hero, natural or civilized? The answer to all of these questions is "no."

Even more absurd than the above scenario is the prospect of a cat catching the eye of a wealthy old man who liked the cat's spunk. Fate intervenes, and the cat is turned into a mascot. Every player believes that if they rub that particular cat, they will play well and the team will win ballgames. The men who rub the cat do play well, and as a result the team wins the pennant.

In *It Happens Every Spring, Rhubarb, Angels in the Outfield, The Kid from Left Field,* and *Damn Yankees* the players are inept, they do not have a good attitude, and they are in last place. Then an inexplicable force smiles on them, gives them renewed faith in themselves and their team, and they are rededicated to a belief that they can do whatever they desire. There is no formula capable of predicting this special law. The unpredictability is exemplified by Vernon standing in his chemistry lab when a baseball comes flying through his window. Just when he thinks everything is ruined and years of work are destroyed, he discovers that fate has smiled on him and eventually the hapless St. Louis Cardinals.

The law that governs these happenings cannot be explained. Perhaps these films then reflect a tone or mood of the culture that had difficulty explaining the consequences of the past and present in a reasonable and logical fashion. This uncertainty left them with many doubts and anxieties concerning the future. For example, how could the people explain the comparatively stable and economically sound state of the nation in the 1950s, after coming out of the chaotic and depressing 1930s and the war-torn 1940s. Maybe the answers to many questions that Americans had about future wars, technology, communism, and bombs simply could not be supplied. Possibly, these films then were a response to that predicament.

Perhaps there was a real need not to have to intellectualize about all the questions that still remained about our nation's past and its future. In addition, perhaps there was a real need to enjoy the possibility of an era to come that would have no Depression and no war. Maybe the fifties represented a time, if these *Deus Ex Machina* films are any indication, when answers to any pressing questions could be left to the supernatural laws of the gods.

Conclusion

The most logical explanation for the plethora of these supernatural types of baseball films, films that occurred at no other time in baseball film history, is that they are representative of those forces that are unknown, feared, and unexplainable. In the fifties, the Red Scare and the atomic bomb provided the nation with a variety of unexplainable and irrational fears. Neighbors who seemed to share in the ideals of the American dream might actually be communist spies or worse, incarnations of the devil himself. It was illogical, but in this age of anti-intellectualism, the logic did not seem to be relevant.

It does not appear that the baseball filmmakers were feeding the fears of the nation; rather they were pointing to how utterly ridiculous and laughable the fears were. There were no limits to the absurdity of any scenario they produced. On the other hand, there does not appear to be any support of anti-communist messages in the films either. There does, however, appear to be messages, transmitted via the courtroom scenes, directed at the inappropriate methods of the anti-communists.

A reasonable explanation for the high number of baseball films in this period compared to overall film production has to do with baseball's ability to reinforce the status quo. As has already been maintained earlier in this work, the fifties were predominantly a period of anti-intellectualism and pro business/status quo. Baseball films in the fifties emphasized non-intellectual tendencies of American heroes. The characters in these films did not question the status quo, authority, or American traditions.

Even Jackie Robinson was depicted as a man who was thankful for the American status quo. Without the help of the men in power and in control of the game of baseball, he would never have had an opportunity to succeed. In other words, *The Jackie Robinson Story* contained very little of the real bitterness that actually occurred between blacks and whites over the decision to let blacks play major league baseball. Even though the film was produced almost completely by blacks, Jackie looks like part of the white establishment, and, by the end of the film, when he goes to the President to deliver his message, he is part of the establishment. Throughout the film he works within "the system" to achieve his success.

Generally, it seems logical, too, that Hollywood produced baseball films during this period in an attempt to attract the audiences that popularized baseball telecasts. The audience for televised baseball drastically increased during this period. Some stations in major league towns had already been programming baseball games on a regular basis. Many major league teams relied on television contracts for their profitability. For example, the New York Yankees earned the largest profits of any major league baseball team in 1951, and 84 percent of their profit was from broadcasting rights (*U.S. News*, May 16, 1952, 16). It certainly seems that Hollywood's production of so many baseball films was not based on the popularity of baseball during this time since baseball attendance for major league games had dropped from twenty-one million in 1949 to seventeen million in 1950, and as low as fourteen million in 1953 (the year ABC began telecasting "The Game of the Week" with Dizzy Dean). The production of such a large number of baseball films might very well have helped baseball regain some of its popularity, as baseball attendance rebounded in 1954 to sixteen million (Reichler 1962, 238-241).

The tendencies that surface in the films of this period indicate that the values of the civilized hero reflect society's values. It is clear that success came to those who played "the game" of life according to the rules established by the greater society. The heroes of this era took life's hardships in stride, used them as lessons for growing into adult, productive members of society.

The biography films and the *Deus Ex Machina* films had one significant element in common. Both shared the lesson that there is not always a reasonable explanation for why things happen. There is no way to explain why some heroes in the biographies suffered career-ending injuries in the prime of their careers and why others had to overcome genetic handicaps before they could succeed. Similarly, there is no way to reasonably explain or prove the existence of ghosts, devils, angels, lucky charms, and communists.

There is no concrete evidence available.

The films of this period reinforced the status quo and championed those who supported the institutions and traditions of the status quo. At the same time some very important but seemingly miniscule changes were taking place in the traditional families and traditional female roles in these films that were to be predictive of the changes that would take place in tomorrow's society regarding these same traditions. Where the biography films reinforced the values associated with the traditional family and the traditional woman, the *Deus Ex Machina* films pointed to non-traditional families and non-traditional women. The traditional family structure would start to disintegrate in the years to follow, and women's roles would outgrow the limitations of tradition.

As the behavior patterns of these traditions became muddled, the distinct characteristics that defined the true hero also became less clear. His values would be challenged as the values of America's game would also be challenged.

Notes

1. All but four of the films in this ten-year span, *Kid from Cleveland* (1949), *Kill the Umpire* (1950), *Roogie's Bump* (1954), and *Great American Pastime* (1956) were viewed for this study. These four were not available from any of my sources.

2. The absence of cursing in these films is an obvious trait that typifies all pre-1970s baseball films.

3. More than one source indicates that Mr. Rickey was not benevolent at all, but rather saw Robinson and other blacks as a means of boosting declining attendance and profits (Bruce 1985, 107).

4. The exception to this is *Field of Dreams* (1989). However, The "spirits" in *Field of Dreams* intercede for reasons other than "winning the pennant."

An Interlude

C oming out of the ten-year period in which seventeen baseball films were produced, Hollywood had apparently temporarily exhausted its interest in the form. It would be fifteen years after *Damn Yankees* before another "true" baseball film would be released, *Bang the Drum Slowly* (1973). An explanation of the use of the word "true" above is in order.

Earlier in this work, it was stated that for a film to qualify as a baseball film and thus be included in this research it would have to meet two criteria: (1) The principal character (or characters) plays, coaches, or has more than a casual association with the game of baseball, and (2) the narrative must either explicitly or implicitly be principally about baseball. A film released in 1962, *Safe at Home,* presents a problem, in light of these criteria, as to whether or not it is truly a baseball film.

There are no baseball games of any kind taking place in the film, and although the protagonist talks about his little league team and the "big game," the game is never played; the team, except for an early sequence, is not seen playing together. The major thrust of the film, which is set in Pompano Beach, Florida, focuses on a young boy's quest to meet Mickey Mantle and Roger Maris of the New York Yankees who are training in Fort Lauderdale. The film appears to be more about how a young boy and his single-parent father develop a lasting relationship than it is about baseball.

However, implicit in the film's narrative is the importance of baseball and baseball heroes in a young boy's life. The film is almost certainly an attempt to capitalize on the popularity of Mickey Mantle and Roger Maris, since both of them were coming off of a spectacular 1961 season in which Mantle hit 54 home runs and Roger Maris hit 61, thereby surpassing by one, Babe Ruth's single-season home run record. Neither Mantle nor Maris seems to do much more in the film than "appear." Hence, this film is included in this work based primarily on the fact that Mantle and Maris' film roles are specifically related to their roles as major league baseball players.

In addition, several other baseball film lists include *Safe at Home* (a 1987 issue of *USA Today* includes *Safe at Home* in its list of the four worst baseball films ever made) and because it is the only "baseball" film of the sixties era produced. Despite *Safe at Home's* lack of "true" baseball film qualities and despite its lack of popularity (gross revenues were under $1,000,000—*Variety* 1963, 13) the film does have utility in that it reflects an era which historians agree was an intense period of mass consumption, affluence, and conformity (Hamby 1976, 231).

References to the 1960s in contemporary America tend to evoke images of individualism, protest movements, demonstrations, draft card burning, the drug culture, and various other popularized events of the "sixties counterculture." Many of us forget that the early sixties were very much a continuation of the unheralded, affluent fifties. Historian Jim Heath asserts that Americans at the beginning of the sixties were fairly content and passive.

> For those with jobs and rising incomes, life judged by material possessions, was better than ever . . . . Most Americans still professed a desire for personal achievement, but their actions often suggested that they were satisfied with mediocrity. The impulse to conform was unquestionably strong and pervasive (Heath 1975, 4).

Many Americans may remember President Kennedy as being remarkably superior to President Nixon in the 1960 election, but for about half of the voting nation, there apparently was little difference in the two, Kennedy having won the election by the smallest margin in history. Dwight McDonald surmised that there simply were no issues in the election: "the nation was evidently satisfied with itself to the point of stupefaction" (MacDonald 1960, 287).

In retrospect, some of us remember that the year 1960 was a critical year for our nation because of the U-2 incident and because of our increased "non-military" involvement in South Vietnam. We might also remember that in 1959, communist-supported Fidel Castro came to power in Cuba. Yet according to William O'Neill, middle-class Americans in 1960 "worried little about military gaps, still less about a flagging sense of purpose. Instead optimism was carried to the edge of madness" (O'Neill 1971, 13).

Film production in the United States dropped off significantly from 1958 through 1968 when more films were imported than exported. In 1958, the year of the release of *Damn Yankees,* there were 241 films produced in the United States. In 1962, the year of *Safe at Home,* that figure had dropped to 147 (Steinberg 1980, 43). This fact coupled with the increased popularity of television[1] would logically seem to lead to the conclusion that film attendance declined considerably during this period. However, this was not the case. The average weekly film attendance for 1958 was 40 million and in 1962 it was 43 million (Steinberg 1980, 46).

Baseball attendance increased in the late fifties and early sixties as well. This was in part due to the addition of two new teams in 1961, and two more in 1962 (Reichler 1962, 241). But the increase can undoubtedly be attributed to, in part, what Alonzo Hamby referred to as a national athletics boom (Hamby 1976, 228) and what Caughey and May dubbed an era of abundant leisure (Caughey and May 1964, 710).

There seem to be several similarities between this era of affluence and the affluent Roaring Twenties, such as the power of big business and the large amounts of consumer credit. There were also notable differences between the two eras. One major difference was that there would be no Depression following this new era of growth and prosperity under a new and very young president. Americans seemed increasingly confident when the new leader promised to fulfill his visions of a new frontier. One of the changes Kennedy promised in this new frontier, symbolized by the selection of the poet Robert Frost as his inaugural speaker, was an increased emphasis on intellectual activism as well as physical activism (Hofstadter 1963, 227). Generally, the mood of Americans in the early sixties appeared to be upbeat and confident (O'Neill 1971, 13). However, this upbeat and confident mood seemed to be missing in the only baseball film of the sixties, *Safe at Home.*

The Film

Safe at Home opens with music behind shots of Mickey Mantle and Roger Maris coming around third base directly into the camera's field of view while an announcer says "Columbia pictures present Mickey Mantle and Roger Maris in *Safe at Home*, introducing Bryan Russell." This is followed by various shots of Russell fielding and hitting a baseball juxtaposed with shots of Mantle and Maris fielding and hitting a baseball. The credits roll as the scene is changed to a fishing boat docked in the fictional town of Palms, Florida.

The boat provides a home and income for the youngster, Hutch Lawton (Bryan Russell) and his father Ken Lawton (Don Collier), a deep-sea fisherman. The older Lawton's work keeps him from attending Hutch's little league baseball games. As much as Hutch would like his father to come to his games, he appears to understand, but he also hopes things will change when and if his father gets married to Johanna Price (Patricia Barry). "Are you gonna marry my Dad?" Hutch asks.

Hutch's close friend is Mike Torres (Scott Lane). They walk to school together and make plans for the big game that is approaching. They encounter another boy, and Hutch argues with the boy about his father. Hutch, in an effort to save face, brags that his father knows Mickey Mantle and Roger Maris, when, in fact, he does not. The little league coach hears about Hutch's father, and the other kids petition the coach to have Hutch invite Mantle and Maris to their banquet.

Feeling further compelled to save his father's integrity, Hutch makes plans to go to Fort Lauderdale, the New York Yankees' spring training home, to ask Mantle and Maris to come to the little league banquet. With assistance from Mike, Hutch sneaks aboard Mr. Torres' fishing truck and stows away to Fort Lauderdale.

Hutch finds the Yankees' training complex and after being rebuffed by Mantle and Maris, asks a cab driver how to get to the Yankees' hotel. The cab driver tells Hutch that he can drive him to the hotel if he would like. Thinking the cab ride was offered freely, Hutch is surprised when the cab driver asks for cab fare. Hutch gives the cabbie a dollar bill, and even though the cab fare was just twenty-five cents, the cabbie keeps the entire amount and explains to Hutch why he is justified in keeping the extra seventy-five cents. Even though Hutch has no more money, he does little to protest.

Hutch finds Maris and Mantle's room unlocked, lies down on a bed, and falls asleep and is later discovered by the pair. After he crawls out from under a bed, Mantle says in a somewhat lethargic and unemotional fashion "A kid, ... Where'd he come from?"

Meanwhile, it is discovered back in Palms that Hutch is missing. In order for Hutch to get to Fort Lauderdale, he lied to Johanna and his Dad and told them he was spending the night with Mike Torres and his family so that Johanna and his father would not miss him. Mike, in order to cover for Hutch, told his parents that Hutch had decided to go back to Johanna's house for the evening. Mike, who is now an accomplice to Hutch's "big lie" and wanting to avoid a "belt beating" by his father, gives in and tells of Hutch's whereabouts.

Hutch, after telling Maris and Mantle the whole story about his lying and his promise to his little league teammates, asks Maris and Mantle if they will come to his little league banquet. They refuse on the basis that they really do not know him and if they came to the banquet they would be lying, too, and therefore perpetuate the lie. Very stoically, Maris says "When a lie starts, it involves everyone. Face up to what you've done." Then Mantle adds, "Every man must face up to what he's done, if what he's done is wrong then he must undo it."

Hutch's father and Johanna eventually find him and return to Palms. Hutch seems disappointed at his rejected request and yet understands his lesson. Ken and Johanna understand their lesson as well, and Ken promises to spend more time with Hutch.

Hutch confesses in front of all his teammates that he lied. However "the big surprise" is a letter read by the coach, written by the New York Yankees. Hutch's entire team is invited to come to spring training and meet the New York Yankees. After the letter is read, Hutch is proud to introduce his

Dad and "maybe my new Mom." The film ends as the boys arrive at the Yankees' spring training facility and shake hands with the Yankees.

Youth and Aging

In evaluating this film, the initial inclination is to conclude that, of course, a film that has a little boy as its protagonist tends to glorify traits associated with youth or the natural hero. Such an evaluation would be a mistake in this instance, although there are quite a number of youthful traits at work in *Safe at Home* and the target audience for this film is the younger baseball fan (Nash and Ross 1986, 2700). The lessons that Hutch learns and the behavior patterns that he exhibits are more adult than childlike. Referring to Robert Ray's discussion of the "outlaw" hero will help establish this contention.

According to Ray, the "outlaw heroes," what I am calling the natural heroes, "represent a flight from maturity" (Ray 1985, 59). Hutch Lawton's character certainly could not be considered one that attempts to flee from maturity. It is established early in the film that Hutch has already had to adapt to the loss of his mother. His father apologizes for having to leave him alone so much and for not being able to attend functions like other fathers do. Instead of feeling sorry for himself, Hutch makes a conscious decision to take matters into his own hands. Perhaps the advisability of this decision is open to question and is somewhat typical of the natural hero; nevertheless it is not a decision many would associate with being indicative of fleeing from maturity.

Without money, food, or shelter, Hutch manages on his own to survive in Fort Lauderdale. When his father initially finds out about Hutch's whereabouts, the audience is reassured, as is Johanna, that Hutch is a responsible individual when Lawton says "Don't worry Johanna, Hutch can take care of himself."

It is interesting to note that there is negligible emotion, a trait that is typically associated with youth, displayed by anybody in this film. Lawton's conversations with Hutch and Johanna and his reactions to Hutch's problems take place with little sign of emotion; no anger, surprise, or disappointment. The only noticeable display of emotion comes from Mike Torres when he screams that he will not tell where Hutch is no matter what happens to him.

It seems fairly obvious that lying is a major theme of this film. Hutch starts the ball rolling by bragging that his dad knows Roger Maris and Mickey Mantle. Mike Torres lies to his parents about Hutch's whereabouts. Hutch repeatedly lies to Maris, Mantle, and Turner (William Frawley). The cabbie lies to Hutch about the cab fare. Ken and Johanna do not actually lie, but they do not tell the truth about their relationship when the tourist group renting Ken's fishing boat refers to them as married.

A significant issue here is determining whether or not Hutch's lying is mature behavior or immature behavior. Given what we know about two highly publicized national events that involve lying, the U-2 incident in 1960 and the Bay of Pigs incident in 1961, lying may not be a mature behavior, but it certainly is not a behavior exclusively attributed to youth. The creators of *Safe at Home* seem to be making a statement about appropriate behavior after a lie is committed. Mantle and Maris state that once you make a mistake, it is appropriate to own up to it. Hutch eventually owns up to his mistakes in a responsible fashion. His behavior is reinforced when the team is invited to the Yankees camp.

It is possible that the film's creators are making a much larger statement than the one referenced above. For example, President Eisenhower denied that the United States had ever sent a U-2 spy/reconnaissance airplane into forbidden Russian air space. When the Russians revealed that the plane's pilot, Gary Powers, had been captured, and that Eisenhower had lied, he was embarrassed and finally had to admit the aircraft had intentionally flown into Russian space (Caughey and May 1964, 696). On the other hand, Kennedy publicly and immediately accepted full responsibility for the aborted Cuban invasion, the Bay of Pigs. It is plausible that the film's creators were commending Kennedy's action over Eisenhower's. Kennedy's behavior is adult-like; Eisenhower's is not.

There is one behavior that Hutch has a propensity for that seems to be indicative of his youthful tendencies. Throughout the film, Hutch has recurring dreams in which he sees himself playing outfield alongside Maris and Mantle. At one point in the film, Hutch plays on the Yankee field and envisions himself as one of the Yankee players. His dreams are encouraged when Turner, Mantle and Maris see him running the bases prior to practice and tell him he might have some ability to play major league ball.

Generally, it appears as though this film has tendencies that are both pro youth and pro aging. Hutch is, in some ways, an adult or civilized hero, and in other ways he is a child and therefore a natural hero. He does possess the unending energy and optimism of the natural hero, and yet his adult-like responsibleness sets him apart from the other children in the film and makes him a civilized hero. The tendencies toward either hero type seem to cancel each other out, and the result is a hero, much like Lou Gehrig, who is equally natural and civilized.

Women and Society

There are two messages that are very clear about this film with regard to women and society. The first message is that in 1962 in Florida, and presumably in other parts of the nation, cities are safe enough that a boy, who is less than twelve years old, can be alone on the streets without fearing for his safety. Not once in this film is Hutch's well-being threatened.

A second message that seems pretty clear is that women appear to have slipped back into their roles as comforters and supporters, the foundation of the traditional society. There are only two female characters in this film, and both are attached to males. Even though Johanna and Ken are not married, it is presumed that they should be or will be. Hutch wants to know if they are going to be married and encourages them to be married at the end of the film. It is clear that Hutch believes that men and women are supposed to be married.

There is one particular scene where dialogue between the cabbie and the hotel doorman serves to further emphasize the role of women in 1962. Hutch tells Turner that the cabbie is his father. The doorman who is the cabbie's future brother-in-law overhears this and questions the cabbie.

Doorman: You didn't tell my sis you were married before.
Cabbie: I'm married? Who said I was married?
Doorman: That's the way most people get kids, ain't it Joe?

This conversation obviously is commenting upon proper sexual codes in 1962.

The only other female in the film is Mrs. Torres whose primary role is to look after the kids, i.e., "Finish your milk before you go to school, Mike." While it is true that Johanna has a supervisory position with the local fishing industry, her role is still primarily supportive. She makes sure that Ken gets the word about the ideal fishing spots being reported by the other fishermen, and she travels with him virtually everywhere. Johanna's work suggests that the woman working outside the home is becoming more common in baseball films.

While the film attempts to show the importance of individualism through the characterization of Hutch's independence, it is the demands placed on Hutch by society that cause him to lie and that subsequently supply the motivation for the rest of the film. If Hutch had not tried so hard to conform to the expectations of his teammates, then he would not have been compelled to lie. Once he did lie, he saw that the only thing that would get him accepted into society was to bring Mantle and Maris to Palms. At no time did Hutch consider not conforming to society's demands as an alternative to his behavior. Like the protagonists of the previous decade and like the general attitude of that era, Hutch was outer-directed rather than inner-directed. It seems fair to conclude that the civilized hero tendencies, with respect to women and society, are developed in this film more than natural hero tendencies. There seems to be very little conflict in this film between the two tendencies. The opportunities are certainly available for Hutch to be an individual, like the person his father seems to represent, i.e., he lives on a boat; he is not married; he is raising a child; and he does not go to little league games like other fathers, yet Hutch wants most of all to be accepted and liked by his peers. He wants to be like them, a part of the status quo.

Politics and Law

It is absolutely clear in Safe at Home that there are no law officials or law enforcement anywhere. Hutch somehow gets into Maris and Mantle's hotel room. It is assumed that he must have broken in, yet he is not punished. Later that night, he breaks into the Yankee training complex and sets off the sprinkling system, some fireworks, and the scoreboard, but nobody catches him and again he is not punished. It seems logical to assume that Hutch's Dad would have called the police once he was discovered missing, but this is not the case. The absence of any legal representatives reaffirms what was maintained earlier in this chapter: the streets of the world depicted in this film are safe and a safe community needs no law enforcement officials.

It is probable, however, that Maris and Mantle could be symbolic of the film's law enforcement officials. Since Hutch seems to be working outside the law, with his lying, his breaking into unauthorized areas, and his unauthorized journey away from home, it appears to be Maris and Mantle's role to set him straight. Their message to Hutch is to work within the system; tell the truth; face up to what you have done. Their advice seems to confirm the civilized hero tendencies. In the final analysis, when Hutch tells the truth to his teammates and his parents, he is rewarded by the invitation letter and the possibility of the marriage of his father and Johanna.

Conclusion

It is with a great deal of caution that evaluation of this film is made with regards to the natural hero tendencies and official hero tendencies and their relevance to contemporary popular attitudes. It seems somewhat inappropriate to overgeneralize from the tendencies of one film of this stature to the tendencies of the larger society. However, if Safe at Home is an indication of the popular attitudes and tendencies of 1962, then it must be concluded that the civilized hero tendencies more accurately reflect the era than do natural hero tendencies. There are, however, conflicting messages and images, and therefore, the concluding interpretations seem somewhat muddled.

Hutch appears to be very independent and individualistic, which is more characteristic of the natural hero. Yet his independence is primarily motivated by wanting to be accepted into the "civilized society" of his little league peers, which is more characteristic of the civilized hero and an other-directed society. Hutch is ultimately not accepted by his peers until he follows the proper codes and proves himself worthy by organizing the appearance of Mantle and Maris. What Hutch's peers think of him and what they think of his father seems to be the most important factor in his decision to seek out Maris and Mantle.

The entire lying theme in this film, which is primarily attributed to Hutch, does not belong in the natural hero tradition. The natural heroes, to this point, have usually been honest above all else, even when it got them into trouble. Lying has, to this point in baseball films, been associated with the civilized hero. When Lou Gehrig told the lie to his mother, he was punished by her anger, but, more importantly, it marked the point from which he became the civilized man. Typically, the natural hero is true to himself and to those around him. Because of his lying, Hutch is destined to be the civilized hero.

Hutch, being persuaded by Mantle and Maris to own up to his lies, does confess at the end of the film that he made a mistake in judgment. A legitimate interpretation of this action could be that it represents an attempt by the filmmakers to align the film with the natural hero tendency of telling the truth.

In light of Kennedy's confession following the Bay of Pigs, the action would also seem to represent an alignment with popular attitudes of the era. Caughey and May assert that after Kennedy claimed responsibility for the failed operation and offered only that the United States would "profit from this lesson," his popularity actually increased.

> . . . the public generally seemed to sympathize with Kennedy and admire him for owning up to a mistake. The press was unusually friendly, and opinion polls showed the President's popularity on the rise (Caughey and May 1964, 719).

Kennedy's method for handling the situation certainly provides contrast when compared to the handling of the U-2 incident by Eisenhower. Kennedy's method is more characteristic of the natural hero, and Eisenhower's is more characteristic of the civilized hero. This is not to suggest that Kennedy was cut from the tradition of the natural hero, but rather he possessed more natural hero tendencies than did his predecessor.

Along this same line of reasoning, *Safe at Home* suggests that popular American values in the early sixties were very similar to those of the previous decade. The civilized hero ruled the day. Authority was not questioned, nor was the status quo. Yet, *Safe at Home*, in the final analysis, might show signs of change that would indicate a desire to move back to the natural hero tradition. Eleven years would pass and another American fought-war would end before the above hypothesis could be tested.

Note

1. By the early 1960s 90 percent of American homes had television (Caughey and May 1964, 711).

The Bad News Bears and the
Bad News Seventies

It was the best of times, it was the worst of times, it was the age of wisdom, it was the age of foolishness, it was the epoch of belief, it was the epoch of incredulity, it was the season of light, it was the season of darkness, it was the spring of hope, it was the winter of despair, . . . (Dickens 1948, 3)

In the eleven years that passed before the beginning of the next film period, marked by the release of *Bang the Drum Slowly* (1973), our nation experienced a wide range of ups and downs which, in retrospect, seem incomprehensible. The fact that our democratic form of government survived through it all seems even more astonishing.

The hope of the new frontier that President Kennedy had promised in 1960 ended surprisingly and abruptly in 1963 with an assassin's bullet in Dallas, Texas. Almost immediately after his death, under the leadership of President Johnson, we immersed ourselves in a war against the spread of communism, a war that 1972 Democratic presidential candidate, George McGovern, called "The cruelest, most barbaric, and most stupid war in our national history" (Newman 1973, 277). It was a war in which the total number of troops deployed reached as many as a half million. It was a war that lasted over eight years, and yet American officials debated whether or not to call it a war. It was a war that brought the youth of the nation together, but divided them from their parents and the government (Hamby 1976, 253). It was a war that precipitated unrest and rioting on our nation's college campuses and city streets.

In 1975, when it was all over, very few really seemed to care about whether or not we had won, the returning veterans, or little of anything else except, maybe, inflation (Manning 1984, 183). With his call for "A great society," President Johnson fulfilled his promise to follow through with much of the legislation that Kennedy had proposed. The Civil Rights Acts of 1964 and 1965 were passed, guaranteeing the black population opportunities for housing, education, and employment, opportunities previously denied them. Education, medical assistance for the elderly, and welfare programs also improved under Johnson's Administration. But by 1968, Johnson decided not to seek re-election. For anti-war advocates, this announcement was the only good news they would hear in 1968.

In April, the Reverend Martin Luther King, Jr., was assassinated. In June, Democratic presidential candidate Robert Kennedy was assassinated. In August, while America watched on their television screens, demonstrators, protestors, rioters, and innocent bystanders were beaten with night sticks and gassed by the Chicago police as the Democratic National Convention, just walking distance away, was nominating Vice-President Hubert Humphery for President. Juxtaposed with these brutal and uncivilized events was a major accomplishment of an advanced civilization. Before the end of the year, the Apollo astronauts circled the moon.

President Nixon won the 1968 election and immediately began to decrease the bulging number of American troops in Vietnam. During his administration, the voting age was lowered to eighteen, the war came to an end, our warriors came home, diplomatic relations were initiated with China, the policy of détente with the Soviet Union began, and a return to law and order and traditional values was sought as a cure for the ills of our nation's unrest.

In 1970, on two different college campuses, students were killed by the National Guard who were called upon to restore order on campuses where students were protesting the war. In an attempt to rid the nation of subversives, and under the guise of law and order, the Nixon Administration encouraged illegal acts like wire-taps, no-knock raids, midnight raids and illegal arrests that infringed on the individual freedoms guaranteed by the constitution (Reichley 1981, 253). Vice-President Spiro Agnew praised the patriotic zeal of a group of New York construction workers who clubbed and beat a group of long-haired Manhattan students (Hamby 1976, 339). In addition, the Nixon Administration attempted to restrict journalistic freedoms guaranteed by the constitution.[1]

Hoisted by their own petard, Agnew and Nixon were eventually forced to resign from office; Agnew for income tax evasion from his home state of Maryland, and Nixon for his role in the now infamous Watergate scandal. When Nixon left office, unemployment was the highest it had been since the Depression (Kolko 1976, 324), divorce rates were up, marriage rates were down, inflation was high, there was an energy shortage, participation in politics and voting was low, and more women were working out of the home than ever before in an attempt to keep the family afloat (Nugent 1981, 134). When Gerald Ford was sworn in as President of the United Sates in 1974, the dominant mood of the nation's people was of weariness, cynicism, and fear (Hamby 1976, 390).

Historian Alonzo Hamby asserts that in the seventies, Americans learned the price of the affluent sixties and, with Ford, were relieved just to have a leader they could trust.

> For ten years the country had suffered presidents who were secretive, devious, and rather openly neurotic. The new chief executive cultivated an image of openness and candor and compared himself to Harry S. Truman as a leader who should be honest with the people and let the chips fall where they might (Hamby 1976, 385).

On another scene, the average weekly attendance for feature films dropped by more than 50 percent from 1966 to 1967 and, in spite of the fact that the number of feature films produced and released in the United States in 1975 and 1976 was more than double the number of a decade earlier, the average weekly movie attendance remained relatively low throughout the seventies (Steinberg 1980, 42-46).

The Films

After an eleven-year absence of baseball films in the United States, production increased noticeably in the 1970s. The first baseball film released in the seventies, *Bang the Drum Slowly* (1973), was undoubtedly influenced by the Vietnam War. In this film, a young ballplayer, who has survived several life-threatening crises, including combat in the Vietnam War, is stricken with Hodgkin's disease and struggles to find an understanding or an explanation for his eventual death. *Bang the Drum Slowly* grossed under $1 million for the year (*Variety* 1974, 19, 60). Even though the film was not a financial success, it did receive favorable reviews (Kaufmann 1973, 24) and it has utility and application for the analysis of the seventies era presented in this chapter. It is not, however, the representative film of the period.

There are five other films included in this period which ends in 1978: *The Bad News Bears* (1976), *Bingo Long Traveling All-Stars and Motor Kings* (1976), *The Bad News Bears in Breaking Training* (1977), *The Bad News Bears Go to Japan* (1978), and *Here Come the Tigers* (1978). At least three elements are common to all of these films: (1) attention devoted to acquiring immediate and future financial stability, (2) a tendency to openly question authority, and (3) an overt concern and sensitivity for the welfare of group members/teammates. Before discussing the films in regards to youth and aging, society and women, and politics and law, some examples of these commonalities are offered to illustrate the appropriateness of the selection of

The Bad News Bears as the representative film for this period.

Financial Stability

Henry Wiggen (Michael Moriarty), the New York Mammoths' star pitcher in *Bang the Drum Slowly*, sells insurance in the off-season and repeatedly converses with his teammates, including the dying Bruce Pearson (Robert De Niro), on the importance of planning for their future financial security. He attempts to convince them that by purchasing an annuity from his insurance agency, he can provide them with this security. As the film begins, Wiggen is a contract hold-out. He will not agree to play baseball for the Mammoths until they give him a larger contract.

Further examples of financial awareness and economic concern occur in *The Bad News Bears* and in *Bingo Long*. Morris Buttermaker (Walter Matthau) agrees to coach the Bears only because he is paid. He will not start coaching until his paycheck is signed in advance. When he finds Amanda Whurlitzer (Tatum O'Neal), his eleven year-old star pitcher, she is busy hawking Hollywood maps of the star's homes to tourists who pass by her street corner. She is only eleven years old and already trying to earn money.

In *Bingo Long,* the entire motif of the film revolves around a group of black all-star baseball players who break off from their unscrupulous team owners so that they might have more effective control of their economic well-being. Much of the action in the film is motivated by the team's ability and desire to earn money.

The repetitive presence of this concern for financial stability represents a significant break from the films of the previous eras. The salary the players received from playing baseball in earlier films was rarely an issue. In fact, Monty Stratton stated he felt guilty for getting paid when he did not play.

Questioning Authority

Each of the films of this period commonly and overtly portrays characters in defiant roles. Henry Wiggen, in *Bang the Drum Slowly*, forces the team's owners and manager to enter into a contract that establishes precedent for future players' bargaining with the team. Henry tells the owners and managers that he will sign his contract, which they are overly anxious about since he is their ace pitcher, only if they agree to put a clause in the contract stating that Henry and Bruce will remain together; i.e., if one is traded, the other must be traded to the same team. The owners and the manager take turns displaying fits of rage at the unprecedented request, but Henry stands his ground until they agree to let him have his way.

All of *The Bad News Bears* sequels and *Here Come the Tigers* are quite blatantly rebellious in tone. The main characters defy the "ruling class" or status quo. Buttermaker drinks beer at the little league games, swears at the pre-pubescent ballplayers, and publicly disdains the company of the people who operate the league. Kelly Leak (Jackie Earle Halery), one of the Bears, rides his motorcycle through the ballpark to terrorize the adults in charge of the league. Amanda asks Buttermaker "where he gets off" telling her what she can and cannot do and say. In *The Bad News Bears in Breaking Training*, the players fire their coach and organize an unchaperoned trip to Houston.

Management tells Bingo Long (Billy Dee Williams) that he and the other players of the St. Louis Stars will have their pay docked $5 each to pay for an emergency trip home for one of their teammates who was injured in a ballgame. Bingo protests, saying that the move was unfair. The owner docks Bingo's pay double for "insubordination." Bingo quits and forms his own all-star team. Bingo and his All-Stars spend the rest of the film in exile from the official black league despite continued attempts by the owners to bring the all-stars back into the fold.

Concern for Teammates

Finally, there is a tendency occurring in all the films that relates to teammates taking an active interest and involvement in the affairs of their fellow teammates. Stated in another way, group welfare is clearly emphasized in these films. It is significant to note that except for *Bang the Drum Slowly*, all of the films of this period feature an ensemble cast. This is a technique that is unparalleled in the short chronology of baseball films. Nearly all of the previous baseball films have only one significant character in each film. Although the films in this period have one or two characters who seem to emerge as the main protagonists, the films, for the most part, actually rely heavily upon the personalities of a variety of characters on "the team" to develop the narrative.

Examples of the above commonality in the films of this period are seen in *Bang the Drum Slowly* when Wiggen takes it upon himself to look out for the welfare of Pearson whom he knows is soon going to die. When the other teammates find out, they too show concern. Eventually a team that was torn by various strains of dissension is reunited around Pearson's terminal illness. Before his illness, none of his teammates cared to associate with Pearson. He greases his unmanaged and unstylish hair, he chews large amounts of chewing tobacco and spits profusely, he has occasionally urinated in his hotel room sink, and most noticeably (and most often commented upon by the rest of the team), he is dumb. In each film of this period there is an "undesirable" character like Pearson, whom the team rallies around, supports, and defends against outsiders, and by doing so, they become a cohesive team.

Group behavior in *The Bad News Bears* is exemplified in various scenes. For example, Tanner Boyle (Chris Barnes), the smallest and the toughest of the Bears, seems to hate everyone on the Bears but takes up for the wimpy, runny-nosed Timmy Lupas (Quinn Smith) when nobody else will. Also in the film, Toby Whitehead (David Stambaugh) pleads with Buttermaker to take Amanda out of the game when she begins to complain of a sore arm. The other teammates support Toby.

Similarly, in *Bingo Long*, Rainbow (DeWayne Jessie) is injured early in the film and starts the chain of events leading to the creation of the All-Stars. Rainbow is hit in the head with a pitched baseball and consequently cannot speak and gets dizzy spells that limit his ability as an All-Star. Nevertheless, Bingo, feeling responsible for Rainbow's welfare, invites him along as the team's accountant and treasurer. When the St. Louis team owner's thugs steal the All-Star team's money from Rainbow, Bingo pays the team's wages out of his own pocket so that Rainbow can stay on and so that the team will stay together. Later in the film, Bingo tells Leon (James Earl Jones) how important it is that the team stays together.

> Leon: Bingo, you stole a car. You know what that makes you, a grand larcenist.
>
> Bingo: I done what I had to do to keep this team together. . . . Bein' a leader, I gotta' keep this team together. It gets real ornery sometimes.

These examples, coupled with the presence of the ensemble casts, clearly illustrate the emphasis on team unity. This theme seems peculiar only to this film period.

By virtue of the fact that *The Bad News Bears* was "the top money producer of the year" (*Magill's* 1986, 157), and by virtue of the fact that its popularity spawned two sequels and "a direct ripoff" (Zucker and Babich 1987, 11) *Here Come the Tigers*, I would argue that *The Bad News Bears* is the most representative film of the seventies and therefore it is the film receiving the primary focus in this chapter.

The Bad News Bears begins with Morris Buttermaker arriving at a little league baseball diamond in California, early in the morning. He pops a can of beer, chugs a few gulps, and reaches for a cigarette. Kelly Leak, whom the viewer eventually learns is a little league outcast, lights Buttermaker's cigarette and rides off on his motorcycle.

City Councilman Whitewood (Ben Piazza) meets Buttermaker, and Buttermaker asks Whitewood for his check. It is at this time that the audience

Tatum O'Neal, Walter Matthau, and "The Bears," The Bad News Bears
(1976). Photo courtesy of the Museum of Modern Art Film Archives, N.Y.

learns that Buttermaker is coaching only for the money. Whitehead tells Buttermaker how much he appreciates what he is doing and that he feels really
bad that none of the fathers can coach the team because they are all just too
busy. Buttermaker does not seem to hear and instead of responding to Whitewood's apologetic gestures reminds him to sign the check.

The team that Buttermaker has signed on to coach consists of a variety of team members rejected from the teams of other leagues. In Tanner's
words, the team consists of "jews, spics, niggers, and a buggar-picking mor-
on." Councilman Whitewood has apparently sued the ultra "WASPY" league,
forcing them to admit the Bears.

After a number of team practices, Buttermaker sees that his team is
probably not going to do very well and decides that he really cannot do much
to divert the team's ineptitude. He guzzles beer and tells stories of his former
minor league experiences while the team continues to be concerned about
questions like "When do we get our uniforms?" At one practice, Buttermaker
becomes overly inebriated, loses consciousness on the pitcher's mound, and
is carried off the field by the Bears.

Opening day of the season is also team picture day. Teams are neat-
ly lined up in their new uniforms sporting the logos of various popular American middle-class establishments, e.g., Pizza Hut, Denny's, and Taco Bell—

all of the teams except for the Bears. Buttermaker is late, and the Bears are restlessly lying around waiting for their turn at the pictures. As the camera pans to the Bears, their sponsor's name is revealed: Chico's Bail Bonds.

The Bears make it through half an inning of their first game before Buttermaker goes to the umpire and informs him that the Bears are forfeiting the game. After half an inning they are losing 26-0 to the Yankees. At the next practice, the Bears show up with their uniforms in hand, prepared to quit the team because of the harassment they took at school. Tanner took on the entire seventh grade because they made fun of the Bears.

However, Buttermaker apologizes, pledges himself to renewed dedication, and orders them to get their "asses" on the field before he kicks them. They obey and after Buttermaker recruits Amanda and Kelly, the "juvenile delinquent" who lit Buttermaker's cigarette at the beginning of the film, the team begins to win. The Bears do so well that they earn the right to play the Yankees, the team that beat them 26-0 earlier in the season, for the championship of the league.

Toward the end of the season, as the team begins winning consistently, Buttermaker begins to change. He starts to develop a "win-at-all-costs" attitude, the very attitude that he appears to detest in other coaches earlier in the film. In a critical game, he tells Kelly to catch any balls hit to the outfield, which Kelly does, but in the process he disrupts the team spirit and causes the team to resent him. In the championship game, Buttermaker screams at his players, tells a weak hitter to intentionally get hit by a pitch, argues calls with the umpire, and gets into a shouting match with the Yankee coach, Roy Turner (Vic Morrow). All these behaviors seem uncharacteristic of Buttermaker.

Buttermaker realizes what "the winning spirit" has done to him, and in the last inning of the championship game, with the score tied, he decides to pull three of his starters. He replaces them with three of his worst players who rarely get to play. When the subs go in, Councilman Whitewood comes rushing into the dugout to persuade Buttermaker against the untimely substitutions. Buttermaker reminds Whitewood that the purpose of this team, in Whitewood's own words, was to provide an opportunity for every American boy to play baseball. Of course, the stated purpose is much too altruistic for Whitewood. Now that the team is winning, he too has become obsessed with winning. However, Buttermaker, guzzling another beer, orders Whitewood into the stands and sends in his subs.

Unlike all the other baseball films to this point, the Bears do not win the championship game. They do, however, win the game of maturity, honesty, and loyal friendship. After the Yankees win the game, they receive a huge trophy and the Bears receive one that is miniscule compared to the size of the winners. A number of the Yankees apologize to the Bears for the way they mistreated them during the season, "But," says the Yankee spokesperson, "we still don't think you're that good, but you've got guts." After a brief pause, Tanner yells back, "Hey Yankees, you can take your trophy and your apology and shove it." Lupas, whom Tanner earlier defended, then shouts, "And another thing, just wait until next year." With Lupas' prophecy, the entire team starts pouring their beers, supplied by Buttermaker, all over each other. They have become a unit of loyal friends. They are able to put the game into its proper perspective by speaking the baseball words that keep many loyal fans returning to their favorite teams, year after year: "Wait until next year."

Youth and Aging

The Bad News Bears is primarily a commentary on the value of youthful tendencies over adult tendencies. Adults are characterized as dishonest, narrow-minded, and phoney, whereas the Bears, the symbol of youth, are depicted as brash, sarcastic, but also somewhat open-minded and, above all, honest. One traditional youthful characteristic that the Bears do not possess is innocence. On the contrary, they are very much aware of and in tune with the realities of their culture. They swear, they smoke, they go out on dates, and they occasionally drink beer.

But this lack of innocence does not distract from their youthful nature and youthful tendencies. Unlike the adults, they do not pretend to be more than they are. For example, Oglivie (Alfred W. Lutter) is not a good ballplayer, but he is good at math and logic and therefore his contribution to the team is keeping stats and keeping the team organized. Lupas is happy just sitting on the bench and being part of the team. Engelberg (Gary Lee Cavagnaro) is fat and is best suited for playing catcher. Each seems to know his/her role. The Bears do not profess to adhere to lofty principles; they are motivated by principles as simple as "life should be fun; for me."

Another natural principle that seems to be at work for the Bears is the "Golden Rule." With the exception of Tanner, much of their behavior seems to be based on a natural or an innate sense of fair play, equality, and mutual respect. The adults claim to have these same values, but they do not display behavior that supports the claim.

The best example of the above contention is manifest in the composition of the Bears. They are the rejects that, for various reasons, none of the other teams wanted. Yet, Councilman Whitewood and Coach Turner talk about the great American game of baseball as being a game for everyone, a game that every young person should be given the opportunity to play. Moreover, Whitewood is part of a civic group who sued the league so that the

Bears would be allowed to play. Whitewood even makes a speech on opening day telling the entire little league crowd how important it is that American youth have a chance to play America's greatest game.

However, when Coach Turner sees Kelly Leak sitting in the stands, he physically throws him out of the park and tells him the ballfield is for ball-players and not juvenile delinquents. Similarly, when Buttermaker inserts three of his weakest players into the lineup in the championship game, White-wood charges into the dugout and asks Buttermaker what he's trying to prove. Buttermaker explains that he is just trying to follow through with Whitewood's intentions. To which Whitewood responds, "Don't give me that righteous bullshit. . . . We've got a chance to win."

Throughout the film the assertions that little league baseball is "just a game" and "just for kids" are repeatedly emphasized. Once again the adults' behavior is depicted in direct contrast to this assertion. The Bears seem to accept the fact that baseball is only a kid's game. They obviously like to win, but they also realize that winning is not the only reason for playing. For the most part, the Bears are a free-wheeling, fun-loving group of kids who play the game for various reasons other than winning. Some play just to belong to a team. Ahmad plays because his hero is Hank Aaron and he wants to be like Aaron. Kelly ends up playing because "some asshole (Morrow) changed my mind." Amanda plays for several reasons. She plays to get the "things" Buttermaker promises to buy her and to show the boys what a good pitcher she is. The rest of the Bears play the game just because they enjoy playing the game.

Misreading his team, Buttermaker tries desperately to win the critical games that will get them into the championship game and subsequently win the championship. Buttermaker is surprised to find that his team is mad at him for going to such extremes to win these games, as he asks, "That's what you wanted wasn't it?" and "Don't you wanna beat these bastards?" Each time the team answers Buttermaker's questions with silence and blank stares which appear to tell him that winning would be all right but not if it means employing unnatural, deceptive, or unfair tactics. The youngsters are able to keep the spirit of the game in perspective, and the adults are not.

Coach Turner's character seems to be the perfect antithesis to the youthful values of the Bears. He treats his young team members, including his son, like young adults, like major leaguers. He even addresses them as "men." In a pregame talk with his team before the championship game, he tells his players that he is going to talk about losing instead of winning, because if they lose, each and every one of them will have to live with it for the rest of their lives. Winning is so important to Turner that he uses illogical managerial strategies like ordering his son Joey (Brandon Cruz) to walk Eng-leberg, the Bear's power hitter, to prevent him from hitting the ball, even when there are no other runners on base. When his son refuses and instead throws Engleberg an inside pitch that almost hits him (a common major league strategy that is employed when a hitter bats after a previous batter has hit a home run or when the batter is hitting well against a particular pitcher), Coach Turner calls time and rushes the mound. He slaps his son, knocking him to the ground and tells him that he could have hurt the batter. Joey seems embarrassed, hurt, and confused because he believed he was doing what his father really wanted him to do, win the game. On the next pitch, the young Turner throws a pitch that Engleberg hits right back to him, but instead of throwing the ball to first to get the overweight catcher out, he defiantly keeps it and refuses to give it up as Engleberg rounds the bases and scores. After Engleberg scores, Joey, apparently realizing that the desire to win has gotten out of hand, walks off the field and is embraced by his mother as they leave the ballpark.

The emotional intensity of the Bears characters is offered as final testimony to the youthful nature of this film. Most of the Bears are highly emotional characters. Even though Amanda and Oglivie are more logical than the others and exhibit behaviors that are typically aligned with the civilized hero, they are both highly emotional like the other Bears and do not hesitate to openly display their anger, disagreement, disappointment, or happiness. Several of the Bears, especially Tanner, seem to prefer fighting rather than resolving their problems through communication. Even mild-mannered Oglivie threatens to punch Tanner if he does not stop his complaining and name calling during an early team meeting.

Probably more than any other area in the film, the Bears' emotional intensity is reflected in the way they defy the adults and the adult value system in the film. Prior to joining the Bears, Kelly rides his motorcycle through the outfield grass during games and practices, seemingly to anger the adults. When Buttermaker tries to get tough with Kelly and yanks his bat away from him after he disobeys an order, Kelly says sarcastically, "Just get out of here and let me hit, coach."

Amanda and Buttermaker seem to be at odds throughout the early parts of the film, especially when Buttermaker attempts to influence Amanda's behavior. She seems to resent that Buttermaker tries to perform the duties of a father. For example, Buttermaker is upset when Amanda has agreed to go on a date with Kelly. The conversation that ensues between Amanda and Buttermaker seems to be an appropriate summary of the emotion and defiant attitude the Bears have.

> Buttermaker: That's the most ridiculous thing I ever heard of. Eleven year old girls don't go out on dates.
> Amanda: Course they do. Where you been?

Buttermaker: Well they don't go out with people like that.

Amanda yanks the cigarette out of Buttermaker's mouth and mumbles something about his resembling a chimney.

Buttermaker: You probably lost on purpose. You probably like the little baboon.
Amanda: Blow it out your bung hole!
Buttermaker: What if he tries something?
Amanda: I'll handle it.
Buttermaker: Rolling Stones . . . eleven year olds going on dates.
Amanda: I know an eleven year old girl who's already on the pill.
Buttermaker: Don't ever say that word again.
Amanda: Jesus, just who in the heck do you think you are?
Buttermaker: I'm yer god damned manager!
Amanda: Big wow!

It seems pretty clear that the preferred value system in this film is that which belongs to the young Bears, and not the adults. The adults are representatives of a society with a moral structure and value system built on lies and deception that they cannot defend or maintain. Even though the Bears lack the wisdom and experience that typically comes with age/adulthood, they show that their value system is more credible and responsible than that of civilized adults, because their system is based on natural principles of truth and honesty; honesty in their emotional display, honesty about who they really are, and honesty in matching their actions with their words.

Women and Society

As indicated above, there are very few attempts by the Bears to crack the barriers that block their entry into the status quo society. Even though their entrance into the league would be viewed as an entrance into society, they actually never fit in. Moreover, they seem to prefer operating on the fringe of the league.

Buttermaker is the epitome of the team's position in this microcosm of society. "Matthau's slouching humanness distinguishes him both physically and morally from the other adults. He is always a symbol for his team's essential ineptness" (*Magill's* 1986, 158). Buttermaker is a former minor league pitcher whose only distinguishing characteristic is that he once faced Ted Williams in the minors. Appropriately enough, he is employed as a swim-

Walter Matthau, Tatum O'Neal, The Bad News Bears *(1976). Photo courtesy of the Museum of Modern Art Film Archives, N.Y.*

ming pool cleaner, an unglamourous worker in the glamourous Beverly Hills area. He drinks beer mixed with whiskey, and he smokes cigarettes the color of cigars. Unlike most little league coaches who coach for reasons other than economic ones, Buttermaker's only motivation for coaching appears to be money.

Probably the most humorous and pointed commentary on the team's and Buttermaker's social standing is the team's sponsor, "Chico's Bail Bonds." Chico's is presented in direct contrast to the more traditional and popular sponsors of Pizza Hut and Denny's. Like the Bears and their coach, Chico's Bail Bonds represents a seamier and more unattractive side of society, when compared to its mainstream counterparts, but nevertheless, a more honest representation of the true composition of society and the Bears.

The fact that the Bears come in second, after flirting with winning the league championship, could be interpreted as another attempt by the creators to show a more honest depiction of reality. The second-place finish, the first time ever in baseball films, could also be interpreted as the Bears saying to society (the "WASPY," little league), "it is more important to have fun, play fair and be honest than to win the league and be accepted into a society that is superficial and dishonest." These factors would seem to be indicative of the natural hero tradition. However, certain issues complicate this evaluation, specifically, the change in the roles of women.

There are three women in this film, Amanda; Mrs. Turner (Shari Summers), Joey's mother and the coach's wife; and Cleveland (Joyce Van Patten), the League Administrator in charge of the equipment. Each portrays a distinctively different character with regards to women's roles. Each appears quite different from any of the women in the previous baseball films.

Cleveland, as her name might indicate, is more masculine than feminine. She has no other name and she is never addressed by Miss, Ms., or Mrs. She has short cropped hair, a deep voice, and no intimate relationships. She wears long trousers and runs the league with an iron hand. She is friends with Coach Turner, and she openly encourages his ruthlessness, which appears to embody the film's ideal of the mainstream adult male. She expresses no desire to be married, nor does she display any traditional female characteristics. Instead, she seems to exemplify a negative characterization of the contemporary, liberated, working woman who is completely consumed and motivated by her work.

Amanda's character shows elements of traditional female roles but, like Cleveland, she is primarily a miniature reflection of the contemporary liberated female, able to compete with her male counterparts on any level. Unlike Cleveland, Amanda is attracted to males and expresses some desire for traditional values. For example, she agrees to pitch for the Bears after Buttermaker consents to buy her expensive designer jeans and ballet lessons. (She asks for braces, too, but Buttermaker refuses.) Most importantly, Amanda expresses to Buttermaker her desire that he and her mother be married. Buttermaker's adamant refusal of Amanda's request results in her crying but only after she is out of his view. She accepts his refusal and never mentions the request again.

Finally, there is Mrs. Turner. Her role is much more traditional than that of the other two females. Obviously, she is married and has at least one child. She does not appear to work outside the home. She is supportive of her husband and her son to a point. But, after Mr. Turner charges the pitching mound and hits his son, Mrs. Turner calls the elder Turner a "son of a bitch," as she takes Joey home. This is quite obviously a drastic change from the wife's roles seen in *Pride of the Yankees, The Stratton Story, Fear Strikes Out* and *Safe At Home*, where the wives are totally supportive of their husbands. Again, this seems to be a reflection of the new female roles in 1976. The new female roles add to the complexity of evaluating this era for natural or civilized tendencies regarding women and society.

On the other hand, Buttermaker's character is quite clearly an embodiment of the natural tradition with regards to society and women. He drives into the first scene of the film in his Cadillac convertible with the top down (a la Shane [Alan Ladd] riding onto the Starrett homestead in the 1953 cowboy film, *Shane*). Buttermaker has been asked to come to save the hope-less, coachless, and pitiful Bears from ruin.

We never really know much about Buttermaker except that he cleans pools for a living, he drinks beer openly and frequently in public, he played minor league baseball, and he was once involved in an intimate relationship with Amanda's mother. That relationship ended when Buttermaker abruptly and inexplicably disappeared. Early in the film, Buttermaker admits to Aman-da that although he likes her mother very much, he is "just not the marrying kind" and admits that perhaps he did not handle the affair very well. Amanda is much more adamant in her evaluation of Buttermaker's behavior, "You handled it like shit." Later in the film, on the eve of the championship game, Buttermaker and Amanda remain alone in the dugout. Amanda tries to sway him into marrying her mother. She confesses that she has already organized a dinner date for the three of them. She then begins to persuade Buttermaker that there would be a lot of advantages in being her father.

> Amanda: I could help you with your pools.
> Buttermaker: I'm a bum. I'm happy that way.
> Amanda: No you're not. You taught me how to pitch. You taught me how to . . .
> Buttermaker: (Throwing a can of beer at the wall; just missing her head) God damn it. Can't you get it through your thick head that I don't want your company. If I did I would have looked you up two years ago. I wouldn't have waited two god-damned years.

There is very little doubt after this conversation that, although But-termaker is attracted to women and society, he much prefers being indepen-dent and free of the constraints, entanglements, and responsibilities that ac-company them. Further, it seems clear from the female roles in this film and negative attitudes of the Bears about the larger society and its members, that the natural hero tradition, much more than the civilized hero tradition, is val-ued and emphasized in this film period. However, the natural hero tradition in this era seems markedly different from that of previous periods. Missing from this "neo-natural" tradition is the naive romanticizing about a natural hero that is characterized by childhood innocence. Instead, this "neo-natural" hero is more adultlike. He[2] is keenly aware of the realities of his condition; he does not belong to the civilized society. He realizes that he survives primarily because of his awareness and because, unlike his civilized counterparts, he knows who he is, what he wants, and why he wants it. He sees the civilized society for what it is, and he sees that joining it is not desirable. A good ex-ample of this is Kelly and his attitude about playing baseball. He loves to play the game and is generally accepted as the best player around. Yet, until the Bears, he chooses not to play rather than to conform to the behavior patterns demanded by the league officials. Another example is Amanda's awareness of sex. She realizes, as illustrated in her conversation with Buttermaker, that there is no reward for ignorance/innocence about the issue.

Politics And Law

According to Robert Ray,

> The outlaw [natural] mythology portrayed the law, the sum of society's standards, as a collective, impersonal ideology imposed on the individual from without. Thus, the law represented the very thing this mythology sought to avoid (Ray 1985, 62).

Using arguments espoused by Tocqueville, Ray implies that to avoid the law, the natural hero tends to isolate himself from the greater society, preferring instead to develop a smaller family or society that is in tune with his own values and that is more personal (Ray 1985, 61).

Almost immediately in *The Bad News Bears,* politicians as well as the little league officials and mainstream coaches are depicted as impersonal, underhanded, manipulative, and dishonest. Add this to the evolution of the tightly-knit Bears as a new society within the league (conventional society) and the remaining conclusion is that this third element further supports the natural hero tendency argument.

Whitewood, the city councilman, is seen in the opening sequence paying Buttermaker to coach a little league team for which he and the other players' fathers have no time. Yet, Whitewood does not want his son to know what is transpiring. (He sends him back to their car when Buttermaker asks for the check.) Since Whitewood is presumed to be the person who spearheaded the lawsuit that resulted in the Bears being accepted into the league, it is also assumed that he is one of the privileged few who knows how to manipulate the law. As has already been pointed out in the *Youth and Aging* section in this chapter, Whitewood's credibility is totally destroyed by Buttermaker toward the end of the film when Buttermaker defies his order to put the best players into the game so that they can win the championship. Whitewood's reaction to Buttermaker's actions makes it clear that his words at the beginning of the season were hollow.

Another indication of the film's position on politics and law revolves around Kelly. He is frequently seen riding his motorcycle around the baseball field. The Bears know that he can play ball well, but they are afraid to ask him to play on their team. He is a mystery and seems to operate outside the experience of the laws of society. Ahmad calls him a "bad mutha" and Miguel says "es su bandido." Tanner adds, "I like him. He's got balls." Most adults refer to him as a juvenile delinquent. Almost no one tries to find out what he is about. Kelly is truly outside the law.

Early in the film he is arrested by the police for riding his motorcycle on the baseball field. He smokes cigarettes, wears black t-shirts and dark sunglasses, and talks very little. He openly defies adult authority figures like Turner and Cleveland when they tell him to leave the field. Through their actions toward Kelly, it is implicit that baseball is not for every American boy. Juvenile delinquents are not welcome in this middle-class American league. The league laws represent the law of the civilized society, where appearances and positive attitudes toward mainstream values and behaviors are the only acceptable credentials for a little league player. Kelly's ability to play better baseball than anyone else in the league attests to the absurdity and injustice of the societal laws.

In similar ways Tanner, Amanda, and other Bears show their disrespect and defiance for "laws" that are based upon faulty principles and ideals. Buttermaker tries to get Amanda to talk like a lady even though he wants her to pitch and hit like a man. Similarly, Tanner the smallest and sassiest kid on the team continues to defend himself and his teammates by getting into fights with much larger opponents or more than one opponent.

Finally, the element of the film that addresses the argument that the natural hero avoids the larger society and instead develops a smaller one more akin to his values, relates to the cohesiveness that develops between the Bears which facilitates their success within a society where they have little input and little welcome. They do not look like the other ballplayers; even their sponsor, Chico's, attests to that. They do not act like the other players. They are not WASPs but rather a sort of "United Nations Team." They have more genuine team spirit than the league champion, Yankees. When Joey Turner is hit by his father-coach and subsequently leaves the field, none of his teammates comes to his aid or tries to prevent him from leaving. On the contrary, they seem glad that he is gone since he held the ball that let Engleberg score.

The Bears truly learn to take care of their own. Toby Whitewood defends Amanda. Tanner defends Lupas. They all defend Amanda when a hard slide at home results in her being knocked flat on her back. They all indignantly object when Buttermaker treats Stein so roughly after he strikes out.

They work together to have fun. They do not seem to be totally distraught when they lose the championship game, presumably because the friendship will continue long after the championship trophy is broken and tarnished. Once again the natural hero tendencies appear to be more important than civilized hero tendencies.

Conclusion

Looking at the comparison of the three aspects of the natural hero versus the civilized hero tendencies in this film era shows that the natural hero tendencies are stronger within each area than are the civilized hero tendencies.

This represents a significant change from the previous three film eras where the civilized hero tendencies had dominated since World War II. The return of the natural hero tendency seems to be appropriately representative of the seventies era in which the youth typically defied authority and traditional wisdom and exposed the false value system of the ruling class and the government. The post-Vietnam and Watergate attitudes and the concern over the nation's financial woes were typically present in the films of this era.

Women's roles and the depiction of the innocence of youth in the natural hero changed quite noticeably in this film period. Women were depicted in new roles, more independent of men than ever before. Youth, while romanticized, were characterized as young adults rather than unschooled, raw, and naive. Their wisdom seemed unrelated to age and actual experience.

The films of this period generate attitudes of advocacy, being involved, taking charge, and asking questions. The post-Depression and post-World War II eras portray heroes who keep their noses clean and do not make waves. Lou Gehrig is the iron horse whose primary virtue is reliability. When he is dealt "a bad break" he does not question "Why me?" but rather, considers himself the luckiest man on the face of the earth. Conversely, Bruce Pearson in *Bang the Drum Slowly* struggles to figure out an explanation for his terminal prognosis.

> Pearson: Arthur, tell me why in hell I swam up and down this mud a million times and I never drowned and why I never got killt (sic) in Vietnam or why I never got plastered by a truck . . . but I come clean through all that and now I git (sic) this disease? . . . I've been handed a shit deal (*Bang the Drum Slowly*, 1973).

Jackie Robinson is so thankful to be able to play major league baseball that he does everything he is told to do, no matter how unreasonable, so that he can continue to play. Bingo Long, on the other hand, rebels when he is unreasonably ordered by the team owner to pay for a teammate's medical expenses, and he has the audacity to form his own team.

Juxtaposed to the affluent and care-free sixties is this group of seventies films that stress financial security. As previously suggested, these films, more than those in any other film period, focus heavily on financial stability and financial awareness. No doubt this was reflective of America's concern over high unemployment, which was at its highest level since the Depression (Kocko 1976, 324) and the rate of inflation, which had tripled from 1965 to 1970 (Siegel 1984, 234). Even the Depression era films avoid addressing the issue of earning wages or providing for an economically stable future. But here in the seventies films, the issue is approached head-on, adding reflective testimony of the popular attitudes of the period.

Most significantly, this film era seems to signal the end of traditional/agrarian natural values in baseball films. The new natural hero is of the city. Except for *Bang the Drum Slowly,* there seems to be no apparent attraction for the rural or small town aspect of the natural hero tradition. Rather, the new natural hero is street smart and learns from his environment how to survive in a world where things are not necessarily what the officials in our society say they are. The new natural hero is more cynical and yet hopeful. His hope, however, seems to be based on a kind of truth and honesty that comes from being natural or true to the self. In this sense the new natural hero still attempts to avoid the entanglements and responsibilities of the civilized society. The new natural hero's attitudes certainly seem consistent with what Hamby asserts were the dominant attitudes of the period, alienation and cynicism (Hamby 1976, 390).

Moreover, the films of this era clearly show little regard for upholding the myths associated with America's favorite pastime. The emphasis upon exposing the realities of the events and characters associated with the ideals of baseball seem to take precedence over glorifying the myth of an ideal baseball hero. The films imply that the individual hero is not as great or as significant as the entire team collective. The baseball films of the seventies seem to reflect an attitude that has at its core an emphasis on the group welfare, cooperation, and individual participation within the group rather than on individual competition and singular individual leadership of the hero. There also seems to be a call in these films for a new order to replace the old ideals, values, and leaders that proved to be ineffective and dishonest.

"It was the best of times" to see new and refreshing attitudes about honest American values appearing after the dark and secretive administrations of Johnson and Nixon. There was a new energy. "It was the worst of times" to see that our myths had become so ritualized that they lacked meaning for a new generation. Further, if the myths were going to survive, if democracy was going to survive, we would be forced to recall the essence of our ideals and then live by them. We could no longer be content to give lip service to American ideals. This, for some, presented a challenge that provoked a certain amount of anxiety. The new natural tradition *demanded* change. Change, it seems, is always simultaneously exciting and frightening.

Notes

1. Most notably the issuance of a restraining order prohibiting the publication of the Pentagon Papers represented a prior restraint action for which modern America has no precedent.

2. The general reference here is to "he," but it could also be "she" when referring to Amanda as the heroine.

A Return to Mythbuilding

T he intense demand for honesty and truth as a national attitude became so important in the aftermath of Watergate and Vietnam that no single entity or individual seemed able to escape the responsibility of "coming clean." However, in the process of stripping away the layers of false illusions and myths and dreams that historically have been a major part of our country's heritage, we may have lost some of the spirit of being an American. Some critics believe that our demand for reality may have gone too far (Poynor 1984, 82 and *Harpers* 1985, 48).

In the wake of the purge lay some of the most important American myths upon which generations of hope and heroes have been built. Gone was the unequivocal esteem and regard held for the American presidency. Gone were those political, social, and religious leaders who unwaveringly claimed to know right from wrong. Gone were the "true" American heroes. The nation's heroes had been demythologized. Moving into the eighties, "polls of the era showed that many people had trouble finding a public figure they even admired, let alone regarded as heroic" (McBee 1985, 44).

By the beginning of the first Reagan Administration in 1980, America's heroes had not yet returned and the "malaise" of the Carter era lingered on. Writing in 1982, Kenneth E. Clark, a Professor of Psychology and former President of the American Psychological Association, argued:

America lacks heroes on a national scale. This reflects the fragmentation and pluralism of the society, which now lacks universal values and beliefs . . . heroes stand for what is right . . . but there is a prevailing attitude that there are no right answers (Clark 1982, 68).

Similar observations were made by other social critics in the early eighties. For example, critic Alice Poynor asserts that the early eighties was the age of the non-hero. Further, she suggests that perhaps our insatiable desire for brutal, stark reality went a bit too far because in the process, we "have killed off all our heroes" (Poynor 1985, 82).

But in the 1980 election, running on a conservative platform that fo-

119

cused on economic growth, a strong family, and a strong defense, Ronald Reagan pledged to restore traditional and conservative values to America (Siegel 1984, 268). Apparently, Reagan's platform touched a "responsive chord" within the American voting public, as he convincingly won the presidency. Some critics believe that Reagan's victory in 1980 could primarily be attributed to the public's negative reaction to Carter's presidency, but when Reagan was re-elected in 1984 those speculations appeared to be unfounded (Burns 1984, 12).

Sociologist Amitai Etzioni indicates that at the beginning of the eighties America was in need of moral and social recovery to restore the respect for institutions that embody our traditional values (Etzioni 1984, 59). The policies of the Reagan Administration seemed to fit the needs of the nation. For whatever reason, the family and traditional values stabilized during the first Reagan Administration. "In 1982, for the first time since 1962, the divorce rate dropped significantly. At the same time, the marriage rate increased" (Etzioni 1984a, 59). Reagan's appeals to tradition were successful enough that by the 1984 presidential election, "both major political parties dedicated their 1984 conventions to the family, values, and country" (Etzioni 1984b, 8).

There are other pieces of evidence which illustrate the extent of America's preoccupation with finding heroes and restoring traditional values in the early eighties. The popular publication, *Reader's Digest,* initiated the publication of a series of articles in 1982 entitled "Heroes for Today." These articles, which continue to be published, are small vignettes that detail the accomplishments of several ordinary Americans whose deeds are labeled heroic.

These same types of "small" heroes were praised by President Reagan in his State of the Union message on January 25, 1984. Unlike heroes of previous years who were highly visible and publicly praised, the heroes of the eighties, according to Reagan, are those who work themselves out of poverty and into affluence or those in the military who carry on the struggle of spreading democracy and freedom throughout our nation and nations abroad.

> And then there are unsung heroes: single parents, couples, church and civic volunteers, their hearts carry without complaint the pains of family and community problems. They soothe our sorrow, heal our wounds, calm our fears, and share our joy (*New York Times,* 1984).

Reagan proclaimed in the mid-eighties that, in fact, "the nation is in an age of heroes" (McBee 1985, 44).

In spite of Reagan's proclamation, true heroes seemed hard to find. Unlike earlier eras, when sport's heroes like Ruth, Gehrig, Dean, and Robinson were plentiful, contemporary athletes seemed to be unworthy of hero status because of their celebrated and enormous salaries, problems with alcohol and gambling, and the amount of public attention drawn to these events by the media. The well-publicized problems of contemporary athletes with illegal drugs make many of them too humanly fallible and therefore unsuitable as popular hero models. The scrutinization of our military leaders and former presidents also seems to make them ineligible for hero status. With few heroes available in these arenas, the nation turned to the silver screen for heroes.

In a 1985 poll conducted by the Roper Organization, 315 young adults from the ages of 18 through 24 were asked to name their heroes or heroines. The results of the survey indicated that five of the top six most frequently named heroes/heroines were from the film industry (McBee 1985, 45). The significance of the 1985 Roper Poll lies in its revelation that our young adults are almost 40 percent more willing to talk about heroes today than they were a decade ago (McBee 1985, 48).[1] This indicates a significant change in our nation's values in the cultural period addressed by the final baseball film era.

In conclusion, there is ample evidence to suggest that in the early eighties and through the mid-eighties, Americans were in need of strong leadership and role models which could restore their faith and revive their confidence in traditional values. David Stern, Commissioner of the National Basketball Association, believes that the American public in 1985 was tired of hearing about the stark reality of the sporting world and their sport's heroes,

> They don't want to know how it "really is" . . . they want the metaphor, they want to see hard work, discipline, teamwork, sacrifice, and heroism succeed (*Harpers* 1985, 49).

The fact that such a high number of heroes and heroines chosen in the 1985 Roper Survey come from the film industry might be even more evidence of America's desire for the myth of the hero rather than the reality.

The Films

There are two baseball films included in this final film era that ends in the summer of 1984. The first film, *Blue Skies Again* (1983), "was an unqualified box office bust" (Zucker and Babich 1987, 14), grossing under $1,000,000 (*Variety*, January 1984). Although the lack of box office success does not automatically eliminate a film from consideration as a representative baseball film in this research, it certainly plays a significant role in this case. The lack of popularity of *Blue Skies Again* can probably be related to a variety of factors, but in light of the previous discussion regarding a need for a return to traditional values, this film seems out of place.

The story of *Blue Skies Again* focuses on a young adult, female softball player who wants and receives a chance to play baseball for a major league team in Denver. Due to the fact that her agent is an attractive female and receives special attention from the team's new owner, the woman is allowed to try out and ultimately makes the team as a second "baseperson."

This film is difficult to watch objectively because it is so unbelievable and unprofessionally produced. Several times in the film, boom microphones, microphone windscreens, and shadows from the boom are included in the frame. Sports reporters covering the team use cheap, consumer model cassette recorders, matching microphones and instamatic cameras. The most unbelievable element of the film is the woman chosen for the lead role. From a baseball fan's perspective, she (Robyn Barto) did not have major league baseball potential. But it seems probable that there are several other female softball players who could have more competently filled the role as the "world's first female major league baseball player." According to Nash and Ross,

> The truth is that there are some marvelous female athletes and a number of distaff softball pitchers who could make Steve Garvey look silly at the plate. But this film will never prove to any real fan that a woman could take her place facing 97-mile-an-hour fast balls from veteran relievers or turn a double play when a 240-pound player is bearing down on her as she takes the throw from the shortstop (Nash and Ross 1986, 250).

Barto's arm seemed to lack the necessary snap and grace, her bat speed looked noticeably slow, and she did not appear to have adequate foot speed. The film seemed to ask too much of the audience here.

Of course, believability and film quality are not necessary criteria for films in order to be reflective of a culture's values. There are elements of the film that truly are reflective of contemporary culture. For example, having the only women in the film actively participating in the job market is certainly reflective of the eighties. As of 1980, "Over 50 percent of all adult women are in the labor force and women now constitute a high percentage of the nation's workforce" (*America in the 1980s* 1980, 179). However, given the circumstances documented earlier in this chapter and the lack of popularity of this film, it seems unlikely that the audience is ready to believe that baseball was available to women in the 1980s. The other film produced during this era seems much more appropriate as a film representative of the early eighties.

The Natural (1984)

In the summer of 1984, the top money-making films were dominated by those movies that were primarily targeted at the teenage audience. The top ten releases included: *Ghostbusters, Indiana Jones and the Temple of Doom, The Karate Kid, Romancing the Stone, Purple Rain,* and *Gremlins.* Common to most of these top films were the themes of supernatural heroes, fantasy, adventure, and/or action.

The baseball film, *The Natural,* also released at this time, seems to break slightly with the pattern of the other top films of the summer. It had a broader demographic appeal, and although it was entirely fantasy, its use of action and adventure centered around the more believable and familiar American baseball experiences. *The Natural* was directed by Barry Levinson, written by Roger Towne and Phil Dusenberry, and based upon Bernard Malamud's 1952 novel by the same name. As of January 16, 1985, *The Natural's* gross receipts stood at $25,000,000, ranking it number fourteen in total rentals for 1984 (*Variety,* January 1985).

Not only was *The Natural* relatively successful commercially, it was also relatively well received by the Motion Picture Academy. In February of 1985, *The Natural* received four Academy Award nominations: Best Cinematography (Caleb Deschanel), Best Original Score (Randy Newman), Best Art Direction (Angelo Graham, Mel Bourne, and Bruce Weintraub), and Best Supporting Actress (Glenn Close) (*Variety,* February 1985). Much of the appeal of *The Natural* was due to a combination of the nostalgic and mythological, aural and visual references to America's game, and to the popularity of Robert Redford in the lead role of Roy Hobbs, the natural.

Redford, the blonde-haired, blue-eyed hero of the film's New York Knights, is a throw-back to the classic American baseball heroes portrayed by Gary Cooper and Jimmy Stewart in their roles as Lou Gehrig and Monty Stratton. Redford's portrayal of Hobbs is accentuated by the roles he played in films prior to *The Natural,* e.g., *Butch Cassidy and the Sundance Kid* (1969), *The Sting* (1973), *The Way We Were* (1973), *All the Presidents Men* (1976), *The Electric Horseman* (1979), and his last film prior to *The Natural, Brubaker* (1980). *The Natural* seems to combine various legends and legendary figures of baseball into the character of Roy Hobbs. The baseball Hobbs' myth becomes even larger and more powerful when combined with the myth of Redford, the actor. He appears to be the complete embodiment of the American myth. Writing for *Newsweek* in 1984, film critic David Ansen sees Redford as the "Golden Boy of the Screen:"

A special hysteria surrounds Robert Redford . . . since *Butch Cassidy and the Sundance Kid* enshrined him as the official golden boy of the American screen. The myth of Redford as the all-American Adonis locked into place with *The Way We Were* — in retrospect, the most indelible love story of the 70s— and ever since he has remained, no matter how infrequent his screen appearances have grown, the most sought-after dreamed about and speculated- upon screen idol of our time (Ansen 1984, 75).

In similar fashion, Ron Fimrite calls Redford an,

anachronism, a star of the old magnitude, a criminally handsome leading man whose face and mannerisms are instantly identifiable the world over (Fimrite 1984, 96).

However, the film is more than a showcase for the legendary Redford. It makes use of nearly every baseball legend and cliché that has ever been told about the game, e.g., Hobbs literally knocks the cover off the ball in his first game for the Knights. In addition, there are many similarities in values championed and story development in *The Natural* and the earlier Joe E. Brown baseball films.

The audience learns early in the film that Hobbs, like the Brown characters, is not of the city. He is raised on the farm by his father who teaches him how to play baseball and teaches him the love for the game. Prophetically, his father speaks to him:

Roy's Father: You got a gift, Roy, but it's not enough. You got
to develop yourself. Rely too much on your own
gift and you'll fail.

Roy and his father practice together while his childhood sweetheart, Iris (Glenn Close) watches. Roy's father eventually dies of a heart attack and leaves Roy alone. Nothing is ever said about his mother. Eventually Roy gets a call from the Chicago Cubs for a tryout. He tells Iris of his good fortune and promises to send for her as soon as he gets settled into his new surroundings.

We next see Roy on a train bound for Chicago. His agent, Sam Simpson (John Finnegan), is trying to promote him to a sportswriter traveling on the train. The sportswriter is Max Mercy (Robert Duvall) who is sitting with a Ruthian-like character called "The Whammer" (Joe Don Baker). Mercy and the Whammer do not take the elderly agent's rookie touting seriously until the train makes a rest stop at a small rural village where a carnival is in town.

Simpson bets Mercy that Roy can strike out the Whammer, a player whom Mercy calls "the best there ever was and the best there ever will be,"

John Finnegan, Robert Duvall, Joe Don Baker, Barbara Hershey, The Natural *(1984). Photo courtesy of the Museum of Modern Art Film Archives, N.Y.*

on three pitches. The Whammer agrees to the contest and then tries to intimidate Roy by calling him various names that refer to his rural upbringing and by pointing his bat in the direction of center field, a la Babe Ruth's "called shot." Roy succeeds in striking out the Whammer and in so doing begins to attract the attention of young fans and a mysterious lady dressed in black, Harriet Byrd (Barbara Hershey), whose interest to this point has been the Whammer.

Back on the train for Chicago, Roy and Harriet become acquainted, and Roy tells her that his only goal is to become "the best there ever was." She asks "Is that all? Isn't there something more glorious?" Roy naively replies, "What else is there?" Their relationship ends when in Chicago, she entices the unsuspecting Hobbs to her room and shoots him with a revolver.

The camera fades to black and then fades back into a shot of the New York Knights baseball team sixteen years after the shooting. The Knights consists of players with the abilities of *The Bad News Bears* and is managed by a crusty, cranky Pop Fisher (Wilford Brimley) and coached by a more reserved, pleasant Red Blow (Richard Farnsworth). The Knights are losing a game and playing poorly. Fisher is mumbling about how he wished he had been a farmer when Roy appears in the dugout, as a 39-year-old rookie hitter/right fielder, just signed by a minor league scout and promoted to the parent club.

Pop, who is also part owner of the team, not only refuses to play Roy, but will not even let him take batting practice. Finally Pop is on the verge of sending Roy down to the minors when he decides to let him play. Roy quickly earns a spot on the team as a regular after the team's prima donna right fielder crashes through the right field wall and dies. At the same time he earns the respect and friendship of Pop and Red.

Red takes Roy into his confidence and tells him of the plans of the other owner, the Judge (Robert Prosky), to take the team away from Pop. After Roy starts to help the team win, the Judge attempts to pay Roy extra money if he does not play to win, apparently having done the same for the former right fielder. Roy refuses and the Judge implements covert methods in an attempt to destroy Roy, the Knights, and Pop Fisher.

In the employment of the Judge are a crooked gambler, Gus Sands (Darin McGavin), and Gus' kept woman, who is also Pop Fisher's niece, Memo Paris (Kim Basinger). Also working to destroy Hobbs, although not directly employed by the Judge, is the sports journalist Max Mercy.

Memo's primary role is to distract Roy's concentration from baseball by seducing him while the team is at home. Although Roy does not let money detract from his game, he is vulnerable to Memo's advances. As quickly as the Knights ascend the league's standings on Roy's heroic feats, they plummet when his preoccupation with Memo causes him to lose his batting stroke.

The Knights and Roy are saved when on a road trip to Chicago he is reunited with Iris Raines, his childhood sweetheart. She has carried a torch for him for sixteen years. Roy tells her everything that has happened to him and learns that Iris has a son. They renew their friendship. Her faith in him restores his confidence and the team's winning ways.

When the Knights start to win again, the Judge realizes that they will win the pennant and he will lose the team to Pop if something is not done to stop Roy. The Judge, Gus, and Memo make plans to get rid of him. Gus throws a party for the Knights who are returning home from a long road trip with just three home games left to play. All they have to do is win one game of the three, and they will have won the league pennant and the right to play in the World Series. Gus again attempts to buy Roy but Roy resists the temptation. Memo then poisons Roy with a special hors d'oeuvre.

Roy is rushed to the hospital where he almost dies from the effects of the poison combined with the deterioration of his stomach lining caused by a silver bullet lodged in his stomach. The bullet was still in place from the gun wound inflicted by Harriet Byrd. He is advised that if he ever plays again, his stomach could burst and he could die.

After Iris comes all the way from Chicago to New York to see him, he is determined to play one last game of baseball. Meanwhile the Knights need him more than ever, after having dropped all three remaining games which placed them in a tie for the league championship. A playoff game will determine the league pennant winner.

Once again Roy refuses the Judge's offer to throw the big game. He surprises everyone, especially Pop Fisher, by showing up for the playoff game. In the classic bottom of the ninth scene, Roy grimacing in pain, comes to the plate representing the winning run. He fouls off a pitch that looks like a home run only to return to the plate to find his handcarved bat, "Wonderboy" —the one he carved himself from an oak tree that fell on his farm yard after being struck by lightning—broken in half. He returns to the dugout and tells the bat boy to pick him out a good one. The bat boy returns with his own personalized bat, the "Savoy Special," which Roy also carved. Roy hits the next pitch, delivered by a "rookie phenom pitcher," into the lights for a home run. As Roy rounds the bases with blood oozing from his side, the stadium lights explode into a myriad of colors until finally the light show dissolves into a shot of Roy and his son (Iris' son was actually Roy's as well) standing in a golden alfalfa field on their Nebraska farm playing catch while Iris watches. Roy finishes where he began, on the farm.

Youth and Aging

Almost the entire film appears to be an exposé of the struggles of an aging hero searching for his lost youth. Roy Hobbs, in his late thirties, is attempting to return to a career that looked so promising for him before his innocence was lost. Roy seems more than a little melancholy when he thinks about how good he could have been if he had only been able to "see it coming." In one of the final sequences of the film, he talks to Iris about his unfortunate accident with Harriet Byrd and implies that his youth/naive innocence prevented him from being able to predict what Ms. Byrd was going to do. He seems to resent his naivete.

Yet Roy does not seem to realize that it is his youthful spirit that got him back into the game. Surely any adult must know that the odds of someone possessing the necessary skills to play major league baseball are very low. It would seem just as unlikely that a major league quality athlete could stop playing baseball for sixteen years, suddenly resurface, and then expect a chance at making the major leagues. Any adult must know this; any adult except Roy Hobbs. Just like the youthful Roy Hobbs who knew "he had it in him" to "break every record in the book" and who knew he could strike out the Whammer, the older and wiser Hobbs appears to be just as confident in his abilities. Confidence is Roy's ultimate link to his youth. He explains to

Iris, when they are reunited in Chicago that after the "accident" he lost his confidence. The implication is that when the accident occurred he lost his youth and with it his hope in the future.

The seasoned Hobbs still clings to and cherishes several of the symbols associated with his youth. He still bats with "Wonderboy," and he continues to carry it in a musical instrument case (perhaps symbolizing the artistic level of his hitting). Significantly, he still remembers his days as a pitcher.

At the end of a batting practice session, Roy is offered a challenge by his teammates. The friendly taunts of his teammates urge him to throw a pitch to a teammate standing in the batter's box. Remembering a similar challenge by the Whammer, Roy obliges by throwing a screaming fastball by the batter which leaves the catcher's glove smoking and the batter's mouth agape.

Probably the most meaningful symbols of his youth that have remained with Roy through his years of maturity are his love for the game of baseball and his love for his father. For Hobbs, the two go hand in hand. In Iris's apartment in Chicago, Roy talks to her about the importance of a father for her son. "A father makes all the difference," he proclaims. It was Roy's father who taught him the game, practiced with him, and gave him advice on refining his skills. Roy remembers his father to Iris in the hospital toward the end of the film when he is trying to make sense out of all the events that have transpired in his brief tenure with the Knights. He struggles to find the appropriate words to describe his feelings but all that he can say is, "I wish Dad could (pause), God I love baseball." He associates the love for his father with his love for the game.

It is this same boyish love for the game that fills him with pride and courage as he storms into the stadium to win one last game and the championship for the Knights. He is met by Max Mercy; Mercy, who has haunted him like a bad nightmare throughout the film, asks him what he is up to.

Hobbs: I'm here to protect this game!
Mercy: What game?
Hobbs: Did you ever play ball, Max?
Mercy: (Pause) No, I never have.

Roy turns and walks away, no doubt feeling like he has made his point. These various symbols of Roy's youth seem to supply him with energy, a youthful perspective, and hope for the future, his own future, and the future of the game.

Roy's character, the young and the old, possesses some of the unrefined and unintellectual qualities similar to those found in the earlier Joe E. Brown characters that are symbolic of the rawness of youth. For example, the youthful Roy talks with Harriet on the train and tells her that his only goal is to be "the best there ever was." Harriet, thinking such a goal is rather shallow, asks Roy if he had ever read Homer. Roy has no idea who Homer is and seems to be disinterested as she talks about Homer's heroes and gods.

Another poignant example which illustrates Roy's rawness, even as an adult, occurs at a meeting with the Judge shortly after Pop inserts Roy into the line-up and Roy begins hitting home run after home run. Roy enters the Judge's office which is engulfed in complete darkness. The Judge, attempting to be intellectually abstract, explains to Roy how it is that he has come to prefer darkness over light.

Hobbs: Only thing I know about the dark is you can't see in it.
Judge: A pure canard.
Hobbs: What's a canard?
Judge: A prevarication.
Hobbs: What's that mean?
Judge: A lie . . . you can see you know?
Hobbs: Well, not good enough.
Judge: You see me, don't you?
Hobbs: Maybe I do. Maybe I don't. . . .
Judge: You're a very impudent man, Mr. Hobbs.

As Roy leaves the Judge's office he mischievously flips on the lights. The Judge growls and shouts for Roy to come back and turn the lights off.

It appears then that even though the film portrays Hobbs as a character who has spent some time regretting the mistakes he made in his youth, it is precisely these mistakes and his youthful nature that continue to give his character meaning and value. The symbols of his youth continue to be important values in his life and prevent him from completely growing up. At the same time they give him power and strength to accomplish feats no man of his age is expected to accomplish. The symbols Roy holds on to inject youthful qualities into his character and give him the confidence of youth. Youth tends to be the value that is emphasized in this film, even though it may appear that age, through Hobbs, is the victor. Roy may be old chronologically (thirty-nine, as Pop points out, is retirement age in baseball), but the key to his success is his youthful spirit.

Women and Society

Without a doubt, the value of women and society is developed in *The Natural* very much as it was used in the 1930s era. Women's roles are once again limited to the vamp and the hometown girl. The women in *The Natural* are not a part of the paid work force, and they are typically characterized as being obstacles on the hero's road to success. Another trait apparent in *The Natural* that is derived from the Depression era films is the depiction of two different societies. The society that is evil is the one of the city where money, corruption, and gamblers dictate policy, and the society that is pure and good is the country or agrarian society.

Roy's first encounter with women in the film is with Iris. Iris is his childhood sweetheart. She loyally watches him practice and cheers him on. The night that he receives his letter inviting him for a tryout with the Cubs, he joyously celebrates with Iris and tells her all of his dreams and aspirations. He promises to send for her and marry her if and when he is successful in Chicago. The screen fades to black as they draw each other near. Later in the film, the audience realizes what must have transpired between them on this special night, after it is revealed that Iris has a sixteen-year-old boy. The early consummation of Iris and Roy's relationship spells temporary doom for Roy's career. The relationship should not have been consummated, according to traditional American morality championed by Carnegie and developed in the early baseball films, until after Roy had worked to develop his "gift." Iris, at this point, became an obstacle to his success. His physical attraction for her distracted his energies from his baseball career and fed his one weakness which would ultimately account for his abbreviated career. His physical attraction for other women prevented him from becoming the best there ever was.

Moreover, Harriet is the embodiment of the woman as obstacle to the hero's success. The bullet she shoots into Roy's abdomen is physical and permanent proof of her capacity to damage Roy's career. It is also symbolic of his punishment for violating a traditional code of morality.

Similarly, Memo intentionally and maliciously schemes to stall Roy's career even further, and Roy still is not aware of the axiom at work in his life; namely, that women of questionable moral status contribute to his demise. At this point, Iris would have to be part of the category of questionable moral status, having given in to temptation on the eve of Roy's departure. Later, Roy seems to know what his moral code violation cost him as he pines, "I should have seen it coming." Iris asks, "How could you possibly know? You were so young."

When Iris returns to Roy's life, she has apparently learned from her youthful experience of sixteen years ago. She has maintained a respectable home life for her son, although how she has done that is not made clear. It is assumed that she, unlike Roy, has had no other relationship, and this appears to be one of her redeeming qualities.

Iris is the prototype of the wholesome, blonde girlfriend from "back home" who remains loyal to her beau while he struggles to get his life sorted out. The template for her character was established in the early Warner Bros.

Glenn Close, The Natural *(1984). Photo courtesy of the Museum of Modern Art Film Archives, N.Y.*

baseball films and is carried through the fifties with characters portrayed by June Allyson and Doris Day. Her loyalty and purity seem to be the factors that attract Roy and get his life back on track, after it appears that he will surely retrace his earlier mistakes if he continues his relationship with Memo. Roy's rejection of Memo after reuniting with Iris suggests what female character traits are preferred by the film's creators and, presumably, the eighties culture.

Iris has indeed been so loyal and considerate of Roy that she has avoided telling him that he has a son. She makes the trip to New York to visit Roy when he is recovering in the hospital after the poisoning episode and ignores Max Mercy's attempts to change her opinion of Roy's loyalty and moral character. (Mercy shows her newly discovered pictures of the Harriet Byrd incident.) As she sits beside Roy in his hospital bed, he asks her why she stood up in the stands the day he rediscovered her in Chicago (just after Roy started dating Memo and fell into a gigantic batting slump). Iris answers "because I didn't want to see you fail." Her answer is evidence of her undying loyalty and belief in Roy.

There is a major difference between Iris' character and those characters like her, established many years before in the Warner Bros. films. The difference is that Iris is an unwed mother living a "normal" life in Chicago. This most certainly is more of a reflection of the eighties than it is of the thirties era, the decade of the early baseball films and the decade during which Hobbs was playing for the Knights. When children were mentioned in these earlier films, they were of legitimate parentage. Even when single-parent families began to surface in baseball films in the fifties, they were single parents by virtue of a death of one of the parents and not from having children out of wedlock or divorce. Quite clearly, Iris's situation is more acceptable in the 1980s than pre-1970s.

However, *The Natural* is very similar to the early era baseball films regarding women and employment. As noted earlier, in the 1980s when larger numbers of women entered the paid work force, about 50 percent of women in husband-wife households worked outside the home (*America* 1980, 6). It seems rather peculiar that all of the women in this film would be unemployed, that is, not working outside the home. This can be interpreted several ways, but the interpretation that seems most appropriate is that *The Natural*'s creators are emphasizing traditional values and traditional women's roles. Traditional values established in the thirties baseball films clearly illustrate that the good woman did not work outside the home.

Roy's associations with Harriet and Memo emphasize his natural hero tendencies relating to women. As is the case with most of Hollywood's traditional, outlaw/natural heroes, the vamp or the sleazy woman is fair game for his affections because he knows she does not expect him to settle down and become part of the stable society. Memo tells Roy that she has been with a lot of men and that she is not looking for any meaningful relationship. She also confesses that she stays with Gus because he buys her things that she really wants and because he is nice to her. We know that Roy has not been interested in any other kind of woman during his sixteen years out of baseball because Iris asks him how it is that no woman has ever "found him." Roy simply responds, "I just never saw the point in settling down." Of course, the natural hero, unlike the civilized hero, would never see the point in settling down. Settling down means accepting society. Roy, the natural hero, is not ready for that.

Roy's mysterious past is also typical of the natural hero. Nobody seems to know exactly where he came from or what he has been doing for the past sixteen years, although virtually everyone tries to figure out his riddle. Red, the amicable coach of the Knights, is the first to try to solve Roy.

Red: How long were you with the Oilers?

Roy: Two weeks.
Red: And before that?
Roy: Knocked around here and there.
Red: How come you didn't play when you were younger?
Roy: I did play when I was younger.
Red: But, you gave it up?
Roy: Sort of; but my mind was always on the game so I figured
      to give it another try.
Red: Just like that?
Roy: Just like that.
Red: Where you from?
Roy: Does it matter?
Red: Do you always talk this way about yourself?

These same conversations could easily be adapted to characters like Alan Ladd's Shane.

Starett: Where you from Shane?
Shane: Oh, nowhere really.

After Roy literally destroys the baseball in his first at bat for the Knights, Max Mercy, the sportswriter, unsuccessfully tries his investigative hand at finding out about Roy. Of course, they already met sixteen years ago, but Mercy does not yet remember their meeting.

Finally, there are the several references to the farm that seem to be obvious references to the natural hero tendency that tries to avoid the corruption, gambling, greed, and all of the other evils of the civilized society associated with the city. Roy is born on a farm and it is there he learns his love of baseball and his values. When Roy and Iris are reintroduced in Chicago, he asks her if she sold the farm. When she replies that she'll always have that, he seems relieved and says, "Good. It's home." The farm symbolizes the simple life, the natural life that is free of people like the Judge, Gus, and Mercy. It is home.

Further testimony of the positive values associated with the farm is provided by Pop Fisher who mutters continuously when the Knights are losing,

Pop: I shouldda been a farmer. Since the day I was born I
      shouldda been a farmer. I love chickens, pigs, ducks. Kinda
      fond of nanny-goats, I am. You know Red, my Ma urged
      me to get outta this game when I was a kid and I meant to,
      you know what I mean, but she died.

Later Roy uses the same lines to surprise Pop of his arrival for the

Robert Redford, The Natural *(1984). Photo courtesy of the Museum of Modern Art Film Archives, N.Y.*

playoff game when he states, "Nothing like a farm."

Roy's retirement to the Nebraska farm after hitting the pennant-winning home run marks his arrival at success, a la *Elmer the Great,* and highlights the emphasis placed on rural values. It also returns Roy to his youth and the traditional values of the natural hero, and, most importantly, it returns Roy to his home.

Politics and Law

There can be little doubt that the civilized, man-made law is portrayed as the most evil force at work in *The Natural.* The Judge and all that he stands for is couched in black and darkness. He prefers the dark. He operates his office, overseeing all of the Knights' activities, from the shadows. His employees and accomplices use only the most deceptive methods to accomplish their goals.

The Judge uses the law for his own convenience. He not only fails to uphold the ethics of his title, but he also thrives on violating any ethic that stands in the way of his attaining money and power. For the Judge and his ilk, the only morality is that which has at its heart the acquisition of money. It appears that the Judge's attitudes toward money are very popular with the majority of the other characters in the "civilized society" represented in this film. The only characters who do not support the Judge's values are those who really love baseball, the farm, or both.

Since those who are above corruption have the love of baseball and the farm in common, it seems logical that the two, baseball and the farm, are being treated as equal or at least similar phenomena. Hence loving baseball is associated with loving the agrarian way of life and its accompanying values. Historically, agrarian values have been associated with the laws of nature. On the logical, rational level then, *The Natural* portrays a very distinct dichotomy between the laws of civilization and the laws of nature. The Judge and his followers are symbolic of the evil laws of civilization, and Roy, Pop, and their allies are symbols of the good laws of nature. It should be obvious which side of the dichotomy and therefore which tendencies this film supports.

Conclusion

To summarize, it seems accurate to conclude that *The Natural* represents a return to the natural tendencies of an earlier film period and the values that accompany it. It is reflective of a nostalgic yearning for a period of our personal histories when issues seemed to be less complex, a period when good and evil, and black and white, were clearly distinguishable. *The Natural* is representative of a much more conservative attitude than that which was reflected in the seventies films. Where the films of the seventies seem to be indicative of a need for change, *The Natural* expresses a desire to reinforce old myths, heroes, and ideals. The upbeat ending of the film would certainly indicate that the simple values of the earliest baseball film period are preferable to those of the most recent seventies. Certainly *The Natural* advocates an appreciation and restoration of the American values that are intertwined with the values of America's game. Based on the available evidence included at the beginning of this chapter, the values reflected in *The Natural* mirror those of the culture in the early 1980s.

It is clear that *The Natural* brings the baseball film back to its roots. Much of its narrative development can be traced directly to the Warner Bros. baseball films of the thirties, e.g., the small town/agrarian values, women's roles, innocence of youth, corruption of the city, hitting the game-winning home run, getting the hometown sweetheart at the end of the film, and generally, an emphasis on natural tendencies. In addition, *The Natural* seems to perfect every baseball film technique and cliché that ever preceded it. There is one notable difference between *The Natural* and the thirties baseball films, however. *The Natural* is not a comedy as were many of its predecessors. *The Natural* is a serious attempt at myth-building. It is a story of pure baseball legend and of restoring the value of baseball legends and heroes.

In an era when the real baseball players have given in to drugs, alcohol, and inflated salaries, Hobbs reminds the audience that the myth of the true hero must be kept alive if we are to feel good about ourselves and about our future. When the film was released, Americans still needed to be reminded and reinforced about the value of heroes in keeping their dreams alive. Just five years prior to *The Natural*'s release, a survey conducted by Cambridge Reports showed that almost half of their survey audience indicated that they were *pessimistic* about the U.S. future while only fifteen percent indicated they were *optimistic* about the U.S. future (*America* 1980, 7).

Hobbs is the legendary model of a baseball hero. His Achilles' heel is women, and that is cured by the "mother-earth" character of Iris. He is soft-spoken and somewhat reserved, although he is capable of speaking up for himself, i.e., when Pop says to Roy, "I'm just considering you." Roy responds with, "I'll consider me." Like a model hero, Roy seems to do everything in moderation. He watches what he eats, rarely drinks, does not partake in clubhouse pranks, and takes the time to show his appreciation for his young fans, e.g., carving the bat for the obese batboy and signing autographs. When Roy turns down the bribes offered him by the evil forces, he indeed establishes himself as a young boy's hero. Through Roy, every kid's baseball dream comes true.

But it is not just the young boy who wants Roy Hobbs to succeed. It is the boy in the old man who wants just one more chance to make a comeback; one more chance to show the doubting Thomases that the old man still has what it takes. America loves the old man on the comeback, especially when the old man restores dignity to the profession. The most recent examples of this contention would include: Ronald Reagan as President of the U.S.; William Paley, founder of CBS, reinstated as Chairman of the Board at CBS and Phil Niekro, the aging, white-haired, knuckleball pitcher as the ace of the Cleveland Indians staff. *The Natural* played on these images as well.

The Natural revitalizes the art of story-telling and yarn-spinning regarding the accomplishments of our legendary heroes. It gives new meaning to knocking the cover off the ball, bat control, knocking the lights out, a smoking fast ball, and "the best there ever was." A perfect illustration in the art of story-telling and fantasy comes at that moment when Roy crashes a home run into the stadium lights. An old man in the stands turns to a companion and, using gestures, attempts to recreate the path of the ball. Without any verbalized cues, the viewer can imagine how the old man's story will be retold down through the generations and how with each telling, the story will grow into mammoth proportions; it may actually have been only a long single.

Critic David Ansen claims that "the upbeat but intriguingly somber fairy tale" is just what the audience wanted to see in 1984 (Ansen 1984, 77). As the evidence indicates at the beginning of this chapter, American audiences seemed to have tired of their heroes, dreams, and myths being destroyed by stories of reality. They needed something to be happy about. Roy Hobbs could not make them forget the realities of heroic figures, but he could help them remember the value of having heroes. Baseball fans, especially, needed the filmic Roy Hobbs to restore their faith in one of the greatest traditions of America. Similarly perhaps, Americans needed Ronald Reagan in the 1980s to restore their hope in America's traditions, myths, and the future.

Note

1. Similar polls conducted in 1969, and again in 1973, indicated that four out of ten Americans polled in 1969 and six out of ten polled in 1973 refused to name any heroes or heroines (McBee 1985, 48).

End of a Dream Decade: Not the Final Chapter

O nly four years would elapse before the next wave of baseball films would be released. They came in rapid succession. *Bull Durham* and *Eight Men Out* were released in the summer of 1988, and *Major League* and *Field of Dreams* closed out the decade for baseball films when they were released in April of 1989. The total baseball film output for the decade, six, equaled that of the previous decade. Culturally, there was little similarity between the eighties and the seventies. As the nation prepared itself for the nineties, several critics offered evaluations of the eighties that were strikingly similar.

"Greed" is the one word that appears to stand out among critics asked to characterize the 80s. "Money was the mania and the manna of the '80s" (Egan 1989). "The past decade brought growth, avarice and an anything goes attitude" (Friedrich, 1990, 76). Tom Wolfe, social critic and author, asserts that "money fever was more normal in the '80s than it was in the '60s and '70s" (Levine 1990). Several writers assert that the character of Gordon Gekko (Michael Douglas) in the 1987 film, *Wall Street,* "is a model for the eighties" (Thomson 1990, 18).

> Greed . . . is good. Greed is right. Greed clarifies, cuts through
> and captures the essence of the revolutionary spirit . . . Greed,
> mark my words, will save . . . the U.S.A. (Gordon Gekko, *Wall
> Street,* 1987).

If the eighties was the decade of greed, it was also the decade of "the deal." Deals that were made with borrowed money. Deals that were made with junk bonds and market speculation. Deals that would eventually lead to a false sense of affluence. For example, in the decade, the United States consumed $1 trillion more than it produced. The gross national product doubled from $2.7 trillion to $5.3 trillion. However, much of the increase was realized on borrowed money. So while the GNP doubled, the national debt tripled from $909 billion to $2.9 trillion. At the beginning of the decade, the United States was the world's largest creditor. By the beginning of 1990, the United States was the world's largest debtor (Friedrich 1990, 76).

The "greed is good" attitude was never more apparent to Americans than when some of the real "heavyweight" financial dealers and their illegal schemes were made public. For example, it was discovered that Pentagon officials had paid $7,622 for a coffee machine, $400 for a hammer and overpaid for many other common items. Lieutenant Colonel Ollie North illegally diverted funds to the contras in Nicaragua from the sale of weapons to the Iranians. Ivan Boesky and Michael Miliken were just two of the more notorious junk bond dealers to go down at the hands of the Security and Exchange Commission. Finally, the Savings and Loan scandal, one of the major byproducts of President Reagan's deregulation policy, will cost generations of American taxpayers an estimated $150—200 billion (Friedrich 1990, 77). "By the end of the decade, wretched excess . . . seemed as dated as Beta cassettes . . . time and family (became) the most valued commodities" (Levine 1990, 113).

But "the family" at the beginning of the nineties had gone through some recognizable transformations in the eighties. The ideal or myth of the traditional American family was still a popular image, but the real American family defied categorization and definition. According to Jerrold Footlick:

> The American family does not exist. Rather we are creating many American families, of diverse styles and shapes. In unprecedented numbers, our families are unalike: We have fathers working while mothers keep house; fathers and mothers both working away from home; single parents; second marriages bringing children together from unrelated backgrounds; childless couples; unmarried couples; gay and lesbian parents. We are living through a period of historic change in American family life. (Footlick 1990, 15).

Many Americans struggled to maintain traditional family values that had been passed on to them, but the struggle became increasingly more difficult. The quality of the average American's standard of living continued to rise through the decade, and with the increase came higher costs and more consumer goods. A sampling of economic cultural data illustrates the financial difficulties of the American family from the beginning of the decade to its close. The average single-family home increased in excess of $30,000 (Miller 1989, 55). The cost of health insurance, automobiles, and child care increased noticeably. The average cost for a four-year college education at a public college in 1989 exceeded $30,000 (Quinn 1990, 104). Finally, there were the expenses of the gadgets of the 80s: microwave ovens, VCRs, Nintendos, cellular phones, satellite dishes, hot tubs, personal computers, Walk-mans, and compact discs.

The financial demands on contemporary American families resulted in an increase in the number of mothers in the out-of-the-home work force. Only one-third of the mothers with children under the age of eighteen worked full-time within the home (Footlick 1990, 16). It is interesting to note that while it may be true that the double income family became the norm, it is also true that ideally, Americans generally believed that one parent should be home raising the children.

In a Gallup poll conducted for *Newsweek*, 68 percent of the 757 adult respondents stated that it was more important "to make some financial sacrifices so that one parent can stay home to raise the children" than it was "to have both parents working so the family could benefit from the highest possible income" (Footlick 1990, 18). This discrepancy between attitude and behavior seems to indicate that American families still placed a significant value on the "traditional family" but were caught up in the rewards of the double income. Dr. Benjamin Spock, the quintessential baby doctor of the sixties and seventies generation, asserts:

> By far, the most disturbing force in America today . . . is exces-sive competitiveness. It keeps people obsessed with their jobs and with personal advancement . . . Instead, we should raise our chil-dren to feel that family ties are the most rewarding values; that social, cultural and community activities can be deeply satisfying, and that gratification from income and prestige in a majority of jobs these days is shallow by comparison (Spock 1990, 106).

Perhaps, resolving the conflict between these two competing con-cepts, family-ties gratification versus job gratification, is what made "The Cosby Show" the most popular television program of the 80s (Baer 1990, 64). "The Cosby Show" clearly depicts an upper-middle-class family that has balanced two parents who have financially successful careers with quality family time. However, critic Art Levine argues that the family values embod-ied on "The Cosby Show" yearned for by our nation's families

> did not truly reflect the new crazy quilt of family life. Dr. Huxta-ble, after all, worked partly at home, . . . and was never far away . . . . As for Claire Huxtable, she seemed mysteriously unfazed by the stresses of her massive juggling act: successful lawyer, moth-er, maid; loving wife, friend and confidante. In fact, "The Cosby Show" had all the unreality of a bubbly '30s musical broadcast to a war zone. It beamed into living rooms where 50 percent of first

marriages were ending, inexorably, in divorce, where one of four kids was being raised by a single parent, where half of all black children were growing up poor (Levine 1989, 113).

There were other gripping realities of the eighties that were equally difficult for the nation to address. Pete Rose, Charlie Hustle, a living legend, one of the all-time greats in baseball history, one who had more hits (4,192) than the immortal Ty Cobb, was banned from baseball for life by the late baseball commissioner, A. Bartlett Giamatti. Rose allegedly bet on baseball, perhaps even his own team. His prison term for income tax evasion began in the summer of 1990. Len Bias, a first round draft pick of the NBA's Boston Celtics, died of a cocaine overdose shortly after being selected. John Belushi, one of the top comedians of the era, also died from a cocaine overdose. Fundamentalist Christian ministers, Jim Bakker and Jimmy Swaggert, lost their fortunes, followings, and dignity following the publicity about their roles in illicit sexual affairs and business improprieties. And finally, there was AIDS, the deadly disease that claimed more lives than the Vietnam War. Some social critics predict that AIDS will overshadow all other events when the cultural history of the 1980s is written (Baer 1990, 59).

In spite of the hard realities of the eighties, it ended like it began. As was stated previously in this work, President Reagan sold the nation on hope, dreams, and miracles at the beginning of his presidential term. Eight plus years later, the American public had not significantly changed. Characteristic of the decade was the United States Olympic Hockey Team defeating the Soviets in February of 1980, when sportscaster Al Michaels rhetorically asked the nation, "Do you believe in miracles?" What American at that moment could have answered in the negative? Harrison Rainie asserts that Michaels' question defined the entire decade (Rainie 1989, 92). Donald Baer seems to agree with Rainie's assessment.

> Ronald Reagan and Madonna. On the surface, he stood for fundamental American values that she parodied. But underneath, they conveyed the same Horatio Alger myth: Self-image over reality. Say it or sing it enough, and any dream of yourself might come true (Baer 1989, 97).

The Democrats never were able to construct a dream quite like Reagan and consequently did not succeed in defeating him or in getting Americans to seriously address the problems that faced the nation. Certainly when the Berlin Wall and the Soviet Communist Bloc began to deteriorate at the decade's end, the people of the United States had to believe in miracles and in dreams coming true. It was like a page right out of a Walt Disney story.

Even the sports fan dream came true during the decade when ESPN began telecasting sports twenty-four hours daily.

The Films

A poll of the top fifty-four film critics nationwide conducted by *American Film* magazine asked the critics to evaluate the films of the eighties. The results revealed some interesting data. A sports film, *Raging Bull* (1980), was selected as the best film of the decade. One of the consensus evaluations among the critics was that there were no "serious" projects made in the eighties; projects that focused on current issues or the human condition (McGilligan 1989, 24). No baseball film, baseball actor or actress was noted as one of the decade's best, but two scenes from baseball films did make the critics' list of scenes "we can't forget" (McGilligan 1989, 27). One memorable scene noted was Roy Hobbs (Robert Redford) striking out the Whammer (Joe Don Baker) in *The Natural*. The other scene was Ray Kinsella (Kevin Costner) talking to his resurrected father (Dwier Brown). Interestingly enough, the critics' two choices are indicative of the dream decade previously alluded to. Of course, every young baseball player dreams of striking out Babe Ruth, and probably most Americans would like just one opportunity to have a last word with a dead parent or relative.

Of the four baseball films produced in this late eighties era—*Bull Durham* (1988); *Eight Men Out* (1988); *Major League* (1989), and *Field of Dreams* (1989)—*Field of Dreams* was the most popular in terms of gross receipts ($30.3 million) and in critical acclaim.

It seems reasonable to conclude that *Field of Dreams* is the representative baseball film of the late eighties. Even the title reinforces the essence of the eighties era. Therefore, the focus of the most recent era of baseball films is on *Field of Dreams*. However, there are some noteworthy comments regarding the remaining films that will be discussed in evaluating the period.

Field of Dreams is a film based on the novella by W. P. Kinsella entitled *Shoeless Joe* (1982). It was written for the screen and directed by Phil Alden Robinson. The film stars Kevin Costner, whom some critics have compared to Gary Cooper (Shlain 1988, 27). The film begins with Ray Kinsella, the main protagonist, narrating his family's history as the audience sees snapshots of Ray and his family. Ray tells us that his mother died when he was three, and his father, whom Ray describes as being an old man at fifty-two, raised him the best he knew how. Instead of Mother Goose stories, Ray heard stories about Babe Ruth, Lou Gehrig, and his father's hero, "Shoeless" Joe Jackson.

Like many sons and fathers in the sixties, Ray tells us that he and his father fought frequently. Ray went to college at Berkeley, as far from his father as he could get. At Berkeley Ray did what most every other college kid did in the sixties: smoked grass, marched, and found some curriculum major to pursue. Ray's major was English. Ray met Annie (Amy Madigan), and they married the summer of the year Ray's father died. They had a child and then Annie, who is from Iowa, got the idea that they should buy a farm. Ray summarized his predicament to the audience: "I'm thirty-six, love baseball, my family and now about to become a farmer, but until I heard 'the voice,' I had never done a crazy thing in my whole life."

Ray repeatedly hears a voice coming out of his cornfield. Ray is the only one who can hear the voice saying, "If you build it, he will come." Ray shares these incidents with Annie and explains to her that he thinks the voice means that if he builds a ball field in his cornfield then he, "Shoeless" Joe, will come and play ball. Ray explains to Annie, who is understandably reluctant to allow Ray to plow under their spring corn crop, that in building the field, he will "right an old wrong." Ray goes on to say that he is "scared to death" that he is turning into his father. Eventually, Annie understands and tells Ray to go ahead and build the field.

He builds a beautiful baseball park and nothing happens, until the next year. Ray and Annie are on the verge of financial ruin when their daughter, Karin (Gaby Hoffman), sees a man standing in the field. The man turns out to be "Shoeless" Joe Jackson (Ray Liotta). More and more players join Jackson. The players are visible to only Ray, Annie, and Karin at this point. This is problematic, especially for Annie's ambitious brother, Mark (Timothy Busfield), who offers to buy the farm in order to save Annie and Ray from bankruptcy. Ray and Annie insist that they must hang on to their dream.

Eventually Ray hears another voice out of the cornfield saying, "Ease his pain." Ray concludes that the voice is telling him to go to Boston and ease the pain of a sixties writer named Terrence Mann (James Earl Jones). Ray tells Annie that the Mann's pain will be relieved by a trip to Fenway Park. At first Annie refuses to allow it, but after she realizes that she had the same dream as Ray concerning the event, she says, "I'll help you pack." Ray finds Mann and takes him to a ball game at Fenway park. At the game, they both hear a voice say, "Go the distance." They also see the scoreboard display the statistics of Archibald "Moonlight" Graham, a former professional baseball player. Graham's lifetime career spanned only one-half an inning of major league baseball. Mann and Ray speculate what they think "go the distance" means, and they set out for Minnesota to find Graham.

When they arrive in Graham's home town of Chisholm, Minnesota, they find that Graham had become a physician and that he had been dead for several years. Nevertheless, they find a younger reincarnation of Graham on their way back to the Iowa farm, and he joins them on their journey.

They arrive in Iowa to find that Jackson has invited many of the great deceased baseball players to play on Ray's field. When Mann sees the spectacle, he remarks, "unbelievable." To which Ray responds, "It's more than that . . . it's perfect." Mark has by now taken the final steps to buy Annie and Ray's farm. He is yelling at them and threatening them when suddenly he knocks little Karin off the bleachers and she passes out. Young Graham is on the field playing and senses that something is wrong. He leaves the field and turns into old "Doc" Graham (Burt Lancaster) and saves the little girl's life. Mark sees all of this, and now, he too, is a believer.

At the conclusion of the film, Ray meets his father on the baseball field, thereby fulfilling his dream and hope. As it turns out, all of the "voice's" pleas were in reference to Ray's Dad and not for "Shoeless" Joe. Ray has followed his dream, righted a wrong, and cars filled with dreamers come from miles around to see their dreams come true on the Kinsella farm.

Youth and Aging

It is implicit as well as explicit in this film that youth over aging is a key value. For example, Ray must build the field because it is a spontaneous act and, therefore, it will further separate him from the thing he most disliked about his father. As Ray stated, referring to his father, "He was ancient by the time he was my age." Upon the completion of the field, Ray says to Annie, "I've just created something totally illogical." To which Annie responds, "That's what I like about you." This entire scenario plays against the logic of the many adults in the film, who are not portrayed in a favorable fashion. For example, the other farmers are absolutely certain Ray is crazy for plowing up his crop. Their reaction is certainly warranted, given the struggles that contemporary farmers face on a daily basis. It makes no sense to them that a farmer would create his own problems.

Obviously Ray's behavior plays against his memory of his father who worked as a shipyard worker rather than pursue his baseball career. Ray was never able to resolve the problems that arose between him and his father—problems that Ray perceived to have been caused by the fact that his father was fifty-two when Ray was born.

> Ray: I never forgave him for getting old. By the time he was as
>   old as I am now, he was ancient. He must've had dreams
>   but he never did anything about em . . . The man never did
>   one spontaneous thing in all the years I knew him.

Ray's irrational behavior also plays against his brother-in-law, Mark, another adult figure in the film. Mark is the manifestation of the young deal-

Kevin Costner, Amy Madigan, Gaby Hoffman, and Dwier Brown, Field of Dreams *(1989). Photo courtesy of the Museum of Modern Art Film Archives, N.Y.*

makers of the eighties, who embrace contemporary adulthood and all it represents. He cannot see the ballplayers because his dream is the reality of acquisition and wealth. Miracles do not happen in the adult world of high finance.

Ray has never really grown up. He "partied" and, presumably, by default, majored in English at Berkeley. He married Annie and became a farmer more out his love for Annie than anything else. But he never really chose a profession. He loved baseball. Through baseball and by avoiding career decisions he remained young. Having a farm that has a baseball field where all the greats could play anytime they wanted and where he could watch baseball anytime was like Peter Pan living in "Never, Never Land."

Women and Society

Generally, *Field of Dreams* is more in line with the natural hero values than civilized hero values regarding women and society. However, in some ways, Ray is very atypical of the natural heroes we have seen in previous baseball films. He is much more like the Lou Gehrig character in *Pride of the Yankees.*

He seems absolutely comfortable and content with his relationship with Annie Unlike the prototype natural hero, there is no mystery about his family history. As a result of the opening sequences, we know where he is from, the problems he has encountered with his father, his likes and dislikes, and that he actively participated in the esprit of the sixties. He tells us that he loves Annie and he loves his family. Even though he does not know a great deal about farming, he does not seem to mind being a farmer. On the other hand, farming seems to be Ray's way of avoiding the civilized society. He appears more content in living off the land than in getting a job like his father did.

Yet when Ray decides to plow under his corn crop, he is quite obviously rejected by the other farmers. He is regarded as "some kind of nut" and consequently does not fit in with the farming society either. Like the traditional natural hero, Ray is on the outside of society, perhaps wanting to fit into society somewhere, but in being true to his own character, he is unable to find an acceptable path. The only people who seem to appreciate Ray's behavior are his family (wife and daughter), the ghosts, and Terrence Mann. These groups are far from being mainstream American society. Mann, by his own admission, has rejected participation in society after having his energies "burned-out " in the sixties/seventies activist era.

There is one other area that would seem to indicate that Ray's character is from the natural hero tradition. Ray avoids the reality of family finances which is atypical behavior of the civilized hero. He depends on Annie to keep him abreast of their financial status. When Mark tells Ray the hard truth about losing the farm and bankruptcy, Ray either ignores him or laughs at him as though there really were nothing to worry about. Ray maintains his position that something will turn up. It is obviously more important to Ray that he follow his dream than it is to sell the dream. Selling the farm to Mark and his civilized partners would be selling his dream. Ray's father grew old when he sold his dream and gave up baseball. Ray refuses to grow old.

Except for the pro-book-burning woman at the PTA meeting whom Annie calls Eva Braugn, Annie is the only woman in *Field of Dreams*. Annie, without question, is the model of the natural hero's wife. As already mentioned, she takes care of the family fiscal duties; she asserts herself at the PTA meeting, an arena typically reserved for the family females; she cooks and cleans; she is a buffer between Ray and her mother and brother; she dresses and looks like June Allyson and Doris Day from previous baseball film, and, above all else, she is loyal to and supportive of Ray.

Let me quickly review a very important scenario in the film to support the argument that there are generally more natural hero tendencies than civilized hero tendencies regarding women and society in *Field of Dreams*. Ray wants to build a baseball diamond because a voice tells him, "If you build it, he will come." After telling Annie his reasons for wanting to build the field, he asks Annie, "Do you think I'm crazy?"

> Annie: Yes . . . but I also think that if you really think you should do this, then you should do it.

After her response, they embrace. Of course Ray and Annie are deeply in love, but love hardly seems a reasonable explanation for this level of loyalty. A typical viewer response might be, "Is it possible for a woman to be anymore loyal and supportive of her husband than that?" Annie's response is forthcoming as her loyalty extends even further.

The farm and probably everything Annie and Ray own hangs in the balance as Annie, after having the same dream about Terrence Mann and Fenway Park that Ray had, gives Ray her support to follow his dream. While Ray is off in Boston easing Mann's pain, and in Chisholm, Minnesota going the distance, pursuing his dream and, presumably, his identity, Annie is at the farm in Iowa contending with large debts and pressure from her brother to sell the farm.

As we have seen in several previous baseball films, the traditional characterization of the female in love with the natural hero is very similar to Annie's. Typically, the natural hero in these films is permitted to self-actualize in a variety of ways while the woman maintains the family's stability. She is the strength, the rock, the loving friend and forever loyal to the hero. She remains "there" when he discovers who he is and returns home.

Politics and Law

It seems rather clear that in the area of politics and law, *Field of Dreams* is in the tradition of the natural hero. There are two aspects of the film that support this contention. First, and probably the most obvious argument, is that the entire film is based on the premise that dreams do come true/miracles do happen. However, they can only happen if one believes that such things are possible. Belief in dreams and miracles mandates that the believer be capable of suspending adherence to the civilized laws or norms of the larger society. The film's creators seem to say that dreams and miracles do come true, and there are no man-made laws that can dictate the realness or unrealness of the dream. Phil Alden Robinson, director of *Field of Dreams,* indicates that following a dream often goes against the conventional wisdom of society.

> Everybody in town was telling me that you can't make this movie . . . Our generation, the '60s generation, had dreams that anything was possible (Fitch 1989, 62).

W. P. (Bill) Kinsella, author of the book *Shoeless Joe*, on which
Field of Dreams is based, asserts that the book and the film are stories about

> . . . a perfect world. It's about a man who has a perfect wife, a
> perfect daughter and wants to keep it that way. . . . It's a love sto-
> ry about following dreams and making them come true. Because
> it's a fantasy about a perfect world, it has to involve baseball, be-
> cause baseball would have a part to play in a perfect world
> (Knight 1989, 76).

Presumably, there is no need for civilized laws in a perfect world.
They would not be appropriate.

The second argument in support of the natural hero contention is
based on Robert Ray's assertion that the natural/outlaw hero tends to form
small units of significant people to which he remains loyal and protects from
the laws of outsiders. Obviously, Ray Kinsella has performed this task. His
wife, daughter, Mann, and the ghost baseball players are his world. This
world has new sets of laws that are clearly in conflict with the laws of civilized society. Kinsella justifies their existence and protects them from those
who would destroy his world. In a moving speech, Mann argues for Ray not
to sell the farm to Mark and his partners:

> Ray, people will come Ray. . . . It'll be as if they dipped them-
> selves in magic waters. . . . The one constant through all the
> years, Ray, has been baseball. America has rolled by like an army
> of steam rollers. It's been erased like a blackboard, rebuilt and
> erased again but baseball has marked the time. This field, this
> game is a part of our past, Ray. It reminds us of all that once was
> good and that could be again . . . (*Field of Dreams*).

Conclusion

The baseball film era of the late eighties is clearly another era where natural
hero attributes are the dominant tendencies. There are at least two rational explanations for the recurrence of natural value tendencies here. First, in light
of the data presented at the beginning of this chapter, natural hero values
seem to be more reflective of the desires of contemporary American culture
than the realities of that culture. Second, since the films were released at the
end of the decade, it is plausible that the natural hero tendencies are prophetic
of a culture that has soured on greed, avarice, consumption, and general
"Yuppiedom." However, this explanation seems unlikely since the rights to

film *Eight Men Out* were cleared some ten years ago, and since Phil Robinson worked for seven years to get *Field of Dreams* produced. The first explanation seems more reasonable.

It is important to point out in concluding this chapter that there are several similarities between *The Natural* at the beginning of the eighties and *Field of Dreams* at the decade's end. However, two common elements seem to stand out: (1) Emphasis on family values, especially on the role of the father/son relationship, and (2) Emphasis on nostalgia.

Both films exert a sufficient amount of energy discussing the importance of the father and son relationship. Roy Hobbs wishes his dad could be around to see him play, and Ray Kinsella wishes and receives another opportunity to play a game of catch with his father. Both heroes were taught the game by their fathers. It is as though baseball has special bonding powers between a father and a son. Roy joins his son on a Nebraska farm at the conclusion of the film, and Ray joins his father on the baseball field in Iowa. In both films, these elements lead the viewer to conclude that family relationships are an important factor in the heroes' ability to understand his position in life. The development of family values serves as reminders of Dr. Spock's comment cited earlier in this chapter; family ties are more rewarding and lasting than income and prestige.

A related element that is similar in both films is that *The Natural* and *Field of Dreams* are family films. There is little, if any, swearing in either film. The absence of swearing is perhaps not that significant, but given the fact that since *Bang the Drum Slowly* and *The Bad News Bears* in the seventies, swearing has become so commonplace in baseball films, it becomes noteworthy when it is not in the film. *Bull Durham* and *Major League*, the second and third most popular films of this period, contained enough questionable language that it was clear that they were not intended for family viewing.

Field of Dreams and *The Natural* rely heavily on the nostalgic value of baseball and portray characters that long for an earlier time when life and baseball were purer and simpler. Both films emphasize the love of the game for its own sake and not for financial gain or notoriety. "Shoeless" Joe tells Ray in *Field of Dreams* that he loved the game so much he would have played it for nothing. Emphasis on love of the game because of its pure value seems to be aimed at striking a responsive chord within the viewer who remembers the days when players did not strike for higher benefits or ask for $2 million a year to play the game. Like Crash Davis (Kevin Costner) stated in *Bull Durham*, a player was overwhelmed just to make it to "The Show."

Economic concern is one of the elements in all of the films of this era which suggests that traditions developed in the seventies baseball film era continue to be reinforced. It also suggests that the culture since the seventies has had a significant preoccupation with money and financial status. Since 1973 with *Bang the Drum Slowly,* virtually every baseball film makes a side issue, if not a center issue, out of the importance of money versus the importance of playing baseball for the love and fun of it. "Nuke" LaLoosh (Tim Robbins), the rookie in *Bull Durham,* questions why he should listen to Crash Davis, the seasoned minor leaguer: "I'm the guy drivin' the Porsche, " says LaLoosh. LaLoosh sees the Porsche as proof of his success, and Davis sees it as proof that LaLoosh does not respect the game.

Without question, the main premise of *Eight Men Out* is money. The film is somewhat of a docudrama about the real Chicago Black Sox, some of whom allegedly threw the 1919 World Series. Not so obvious is the economic issue in *Major League.* The female owner of the Cleveland Indians intends to construct a team so bad that the team will be forced to move to a sunnier location, and in the process she will make a large amount of money from the incentives offered by Florida businessmen. She has no knowledge or fondness of the game. However, her plan backfires as the team of rejects that she constructs wins the American League pennant.

Finally, the recurring theme of the good woman as the loyal female is once again present in all of the late eighties baseball films. For example, Annie Savoy (Susan Sarandon) is waiting for Crash Davis after he "hangs up his cleats" at the end of *Bull Durham.* Earlier in the film Crash tries to seduce Annie, and she refuses stating, "I'm committed to Nuke for the season." The wives of the men in *Eight Men Out* remain loyal to them throughout their trials and tribulations during the scandal.

The main protagonist in *Major League* is Jake Taylor (Tom Berenger), a catcher with "maybe one good season" left, who attempts to reunite with his former love, Lynn Wells (Rene Russo). She fends him off because "He's just a kid who refuses to grow up," because he's had numerous affairs that have repeatedly embarrassed her, and because she is engaged to be married to someone else. However, at the conclusion of the film, Lynn is waiting for Jake, they embrace, and the movie ends.

Despite the major changes that have occurred regarding women's rights and expanded opportunities for women, the characterization of the female has not varied significantly throughout all the years of baseball films. In the late eighties, when more women than not work outside the home (Footlick 1990, 17), it seems curious that the role of the good woman has not changed significantly. Certainly, the character of Annie Savoy in *Bull Durham* breaks with many of the traditional roles of the good woman, but with regard to outstanding loyalty, she is right there with all the other baseball women.

Nevertheless, the newness of the Annie Savoy character is noteworthy. She, at the very least, offers non-traditional characteristics for the good

*Pictured above: Susan Sarandon and Kevin Costner. Below: Susan Saran-
don and Tim Robbins,* Bull Durham *(1988). Photo courtesy of the Museum of
Modern Art Film Archives, N.Y.*

woman. In another baseball era, Annie might have been viewed as a vamp, except she does not fit that mold either. She does not drain the hero of his strength. Her "job" is to supply one minor league player each season with a "certain amount of life wisdom." She tells us at the beginning of the film that she reads them Emily Dickinson or Walt Whitman and makes them feel confident and they make her feel safe . . . and pretty. Annie says, "What I give them lasts a lifetime. What they give me lasts 142 games." Annie is seductive, and part of the life wisdom she gives is sex, but only one player per season benefits from her generosity. We see that in spite of whatever flaws she has, she is redeemed by her loyalty.

Annie is also intelligent. She teaches English. She studies baseball and is a storehouse of baseball technique and statistics. Although she engages in casual sex, she seems to know exactly where she stands within the world of minor league baseball, which is her real love, and within society in general. She has tried all the religions "and the only church that feeds the soul day in and day out is the Church of Baseball. " Annie has built a shrine of baseball paraphernalia and candles to celebrate the only religion she trusts. She is undoubtedly a complex character, but in the end she is the traditionally loyal good woman. Perhaps Annie's character is prophetic of a new good woman's role in baseball films—perhaps a good female who is not loyal. Is it possible?

Another new element in the most recent baseball films, including the one discussed above, is baseball as religion. Annie's testimony is an example of one obvious reference. A bit more subtle reference appears in *Major League*. Pedro Cerrano (Dennis Haysbert) worships a voodoo god named Joboo who is supposed to remove evil spirits from his bat. He feuds with a veteran born-again Christian, Eddie Harris (Chelcie Ross), over their religious beliefs. Finally, Cerrano rejects Joboo and says he will hit the ball without Joboo's help. It is capturing baseball's championship pennant that rescues Cerrano, not Joboo and not Christianity.

The final example of references to baseball as religion in these late eighties films is from *Field of Dreams*. It is a simple reference but a significant one nonetheless. Both "Shoeless" Joe and Ray's father ask Ray if they are in heaven when they first arrive on his baseball field. Ray responds, "No . . . It's Iowa." Of course Ray's reference would make a good tourist promo for Iowa, but his answer indicates that he misses the point of the question. What they are probably implying is that any place where a dead baseball player could come and play baseball anytime at all must be heaven. The metaphor is: heaven is playing baseball forever . . . on a perfect field.

Perhaps the presence of these references to baseball as religion is relative to what W. P. Kinsella said about any perfect world having to include baseball. Baseball in its pure form is purer than today's religion. It is, perhaps, something more tangible to hold on to; something more miraculous.

Conclusion

T hroughout the history of baseball films there have been several noticeable changes in values. The hero's values in the films have championed the natural baseball hero, the civilized baseball hero, or some combination of both. As we look at the development of baseball heroes with respect to the two hero traditions of Hollywood cinema as argued by Robert Ray, it becomes clearer that the products of Hollywood do mirror the changes of the culture that gives birth to the films.

The thirties or the Depression era baseball films establish the value of the natural hero tendencies. The films featuring Joe E. Brown depict simple values associated with the rural or small town as paramount. The youthful innocence and honesty of the hero was an asset that set him apart from his colleagues. The hero was confident, energetic, and generally full of hope.

The city, in these early films, is seen as the center of corruption, as impersonal, and as short on moral fiber. The hero is depicted as someone who is on the outside of this society because of his rural roots and upstanding morality. Generally the civilized society, which is typically represented by the city and the status quo, is not a very desirable place to be in these early baseball films. Yet the hero has to learn to adapt to the city if he expects to fulfill his dream of playing professional baseball.

Women's roles in these films seem to establish a model for each successive era that follows. Women, whether good or evil, are depicted as obstacles on the road to success, obstacles that the hero must overcome if he is to achieve success. The hero is never fully able to consummate a relationship with any woman until he has acquired some significant level of success.

Additionally, the good women are generally depicted as being loyal to the hero while he, more often than not, carries on relationships with women of questionable morals. The good woman's reward for her loyalty comes at the end of the film when she marries the hero and assumes her accepted place in society. These images of the good woman seem necessary during the Depression era to reinforce traditional institutions and relationships, i.e., marriage. In addition, women are generally depicted in subordinate roles to the male characters. They do not work outside the home, and they do not raise children.

The roles of women do not change significantly until the seventies.

However, in the eighties, women's roles once again revert back to the proto-type roles established in the thirties. The change in women's roles from the seventies to the eighties seems to be indicative of a cultural attitude that sug-gests that it is preferable for women to be in the home, raising children, and morally supporting the family and not working outside the home. Surveys from popular periodicals during the eighties decade certainly indicated the presence and popularity of such an attitude. A popularly held opinion during the early 1980s was that the declining family structure could be attributed to a lack of available parenting which was obviously due to the necessity of hav-ing both parents working outside the home to financially support the family. Traditionalists automatically translated this to mean, "Women should stay home and men should go to work" (Etzioni 1984, 59). *The Natural* and *Field of Dreams* underscores this perspective with its portrayal of the role of the good woman.

Children seem to be of little significance in the films of the Depres-sion era. This may be reflective of a national trend in the era that showed a general reluctance of parents to bring children into the Depression era pover-ty (Jackson 1986, 65). Children and families gradually begin to appear in the films of the fifties. However, the protagonist, with his childlike behavior, fre-quently takes the role of the child.

During the post-Depression/World War II era, the natural tendencies began to wane. American society/the city is viewed as the best place to be. It is in the city of the early forties where opportunities become available to any American willing to work hard. The rural values of the initial film period are not an issue. However, the youthful nature of the protagonist is still very much apparent. Generally, the films of this era seem to communicate that in-dustrialized American cities are not corrupt and are not impersonal; in fact, they are just the opposite. Policemen are friendly and helpful. Other Ameri-can institutions, e.g., marriage and the military, are highly regarded and un-challenged. It is a period of social stability.

Women are still viewed as obstacles who distract the baseball hero's attention. Yet, they are also depicted as loyal and in the home. They are pre-dominantly seen as subordinate to the male, yet their support is important for the well-being of the hero. In this regard, their power is so great and so neces-sary to the hero that they might easily be viewed as the dominant character in the male-female relationships of this era. There are still no families with young children in this era, which reflects similar attitudes to those of the thir-ties regarding children.

Generally, the protagonists of this era embrace the civilized socie-ty's values. They are depicted as members of society who gladly accept their responsibilities to society without question. It seems logical that the films of this era did what they could to strengthen and nurture the war effort. Primarily this meant creating a positive image of the United States for the men fighting overseas and their families at home.

The period following the war marked an era of increased baseball film production. Biographies that reasserted the value of the status quo American heavily populate this era. The proliferation of biography films was probably caused by the success of *Pride of the Yankees* and also the need to show returning servicemen how other American heroes had overcome their handicaps and attained greatness. The filmmakers attempted to produce films that would capitalize on both events.

The other dominant type of baseball films in this era, labeled *"Deus Ex Machina,"* seemed to be a reflection of the confusion that Americans had about the strange events occurring after the war. The end of World War II, the Cold War, the Korean War, and the Communist Scare/McCarthy era all led to a great degree of distrust for the traditional explanations for events occurring at this time. The irrationality of these films reflected an historical period which many scholars have described as a period of anti-intellectualism.

Traditional families as well as single-parent families begin to appear in this era's baseball films as do women working for pay. However, women are still predominantly depicted as loyal subordinates of their spouses. At the same time, it is important to note that women's roles continue to be characterized, when compared to males, as emotionally and morally more stable, more rational, more sure of themselves; more often than not, they supply the necessary energy and force behind their spouse's success. This has been true since the thirties films and continued to be true in the eighties. Again, the seventies era provides the only exception to this formula.

Even though the status quo is emphasized and supported in the films of the fifties, there is a slight return to the agrarian/small town values in films like *The Stratton Story, The Pride of St. Louis,* and *It Happens Every Spring.* When society itself gets too complicated to figure out, it seems appropriate that a simpler set of values becomes more attractive. This perhaps has something to do with the frequent reappearance of the natural laws of the farm. Certainly with all the military, political, sports, and film heroes that were available to the culture of the fifties, there was no need, as there was in the eighties, to rebuild the myth of the hero with the agrarian values.

There is very little to note about the one sixties film, *Safe at Home,* and the accuracy of any conclusion reasoned from one very poor film is open to speculation. However, the film does seem to continue the trends established in the fifties. There are no significant changes here. The sixties seemed to be an era of no consequences, of uncanny calmness.

The seventies baseball film era produced some fairly radical changes in the baseball hero. The most noticeable changes were reflected in the roles of women, the hero working against the status quo or the authority figures, and the concern for group activity, the ensemble cast. It is also apparent in these films that there is a significant degree of concern and emphasis on money, which is uncharacteristic of all other baseball film eras. However, this trend continues from this point on through the eighties. This economic theme undoubtedly related to the culture's concern for economic stability. All of these changes seemed to be occurring as part of a general popular trend demanding realistic perspectives.

As was pointed out earlier, there seems to be a high degree of concern for togetherness and cohesiveness displayed in the films of this era. If this observation is accurate, it presents a problem of interpretation because the seventies era has become popularly known as the "me" generation (*U.S. News and World Report* 1978, 40). Yet in every one of the films of this era, even though the individual characters are independent and non-conforming, there is a heightened sense of "other" awareness. An appropriate explanation may be that the concern for others in these films is directed at others who belong to the care-giver's own group. Therefore, the care and sensitivity is given out of a genuine concern for the welfare of the group member and not out of a general sense of responsibility for all of humanity.

Women are not depicted as subservient, loyal, or necessarily "wholesome" in these films. In most cases they are portrayed on an equal level with men. They are employed, independent, and physically able to perform any task that a man can perform. Certainly this reflects the culture of the period when men and women's roles were increasingly interchangeable, both in the home and in the work place (*U.S. News and World Report* 1978, 42).

It seems that a general characteristic of the baseball heroes of this era is to be a maverick. The hero demands more control over his own affairs and challenges the authority of anyone who attempts to interfere with that control. Agrarian values in general are not of any consequence in this era, but the honesty of the simple rural value system is present. The heroes in this era operate predominantly on the outside or on the fringe of society rather than from within. Therefore, natural tendencies seem to be more important than civilized, but then again, any tendency in this era seems to be almost too restraining. It is an era that almost defies the civilized or the natural hero tendencies. It appears to establish new tendencies or at least a new twist on the normative tendencies.

The seventies films tend to destroy the myth of the baseball hero, rendering it bare so that everyone can see that it, like the other myths of our society, is a prevarication. This tendency appears to be an accurate reflection of the seventies culture. It is quite interesting and quite appropriate to note that the seventies produced the only baseball film to date in which the protagonists' team comes in second. In American baseball films, the protagonist, the baseball hero, "normally" comes in first. But as most of us can readily admit, winning is not always realistic and the seventies demanded reality.

As we have seen, in our culture and in our films, for many Americans the seventies went too far in stripping the nation of its heroes. The mythical heroes seem to be necessary ingredients for a healthier and more optimistic nation. Whether their feats are realistically attainable does not seem to be as important as what they represent. The appeal of *The Natural* certainly seems to indicate that by 1984, the nation had had all the reality it could handle from the seventies. The movie audiences wanted to feel good again, and *The Natural* fit well with those desires. This argument is further reinforced with the popularity of *Field of Dreams* in 1989.

Using Ray's model of the natural hero's values versus the civilized hero's values regarding youth and aging, society and women, and politics and law leads to the general conclusion that the natural hero tendencies are valued over civilized hero tendencies in the majority of Hollywood's baseball films. Youth is valued over aging, and personal, internalized law is valued over man-made or civilized laws.

The exception to this conclusion concerns the value of women and society. Typically the baseball films from 1929 through 1989 resolved the conflict between the natural hero's values and the civilized hero's values by depicting a hero who eventually "settled down," in many instances with the idealized, wholesome woman, and became an accepted member of society. As Ray asserts, resolving the conflict between the two competing value systems has traditionally been the key to the success of classic Hollywood cinema (Ray 1985, 57). Ray's assertion certainly holds true with baseball films. Even *The Bad News Bears* (natural heroes) are ultimately accepted into the little league (society) that rejected them at the beginning of the film.

Ray's outlaw/official paradigm seemed to be an effective tool for analyzing the values of the heroes in baseball films. Further, the values of the heroes in baseball films, because they are a reflection of the popular values of the culture producing the films, assisted in the understanding of that culture. In addition, Ray's model provides an appropriate tool for structuring a sociocultural analysis of a group of films.

I believe, and it seems that the new wave of baseball films lend some support here, that with the growing desire of Americans for sports fare, whether on television or through other media, Hollywood will produce more baseball films and not less. Hollywood can, after all, speed up the intensity, heighten the emotional level, and introduce more action than the actual game has to offer live or on television. American baseball fans, and movie goers in general, never really seem to tire of the predictable endings of baseball films. (We all really "knew" how *The Natural* and similarly how *Major League* would end.) It is the development of the story that attracts an audience to the film. It is the nature of the mythbuilding that is the key to the popularity of baseball films. To reiterate what W. P. Kinsella, author of *Shoeless Joe,* said about *Field of Dreams*:

> . . . It's a fantasy about a perfect world, it has to involve baseball, because baseball would have a part to play in a perfect world. (Knight 1989, 76)

It is highly conceivable that the silverscreen baseball hero will continue to be developed toward the natural hero tendencies. America is still in a nostalgic mood and seems to be, more than ever, determined to clean up the images of her heroes. But until it happens in reality, Hollywood will continue to provide us with images of the ideal hero.

Bibliography

Allen, Frederick Lewis. *Only Yesterday: An Informal History of the Nineteen-Twenties.* New York: Harper and Row, 1931.

Allen, Frederick Lewis. *Since Yesterday: The Nineteen-Thirties in America.* New York: Harper and Row, 1940.

Allen, Robert C. and Douglas Gomery. *Film History: Theory and Practice.* New York: Alfred A. Knopf, 1985.

America in the 1980's. Washington, D.C.: Congressional Quarterly, Inc., 1980.

Ansen, David. "Robert Redford: An American All-Star." *Newsweek* 103 (May 28, 1984): 75-80.

The Baseball Encyclopedia. Toronto: The Macmillan Company, 1969.

Baer, Donald. "All the Best." *U.S. News and World Report* 109 (July 9, 1990): 44-80.

Baxter, John. *Hollywood in the Sixties.* New York: A.S. Barnes, 1972.

Baxter, John. *Hollywood in the Thirties.* New York: A.S. Barnes, 1968.

Bergman, Andrew. *We're in the Money.* New York: University Press, 1971.

Betts, John Richards. *America's Sporting Heritage: 1850-1950.* Reading, Massachusetts: Addison-Wesley Publishing Company, 1974.

Bohn, Thomas and Richard Stromgren. *Light and Shadows.* Palo Alto, California: Mayfield Publishing Company, 1983.

Bordwell, David and Kristin Thompson. *Film Art.* New York: Alfred A. Knopf, 1986.

159

Browne, Ray B. and Marshall W. Fishwick, eds., *The Hero in Transition*. Bowling Green, Ohio: Bowling Green State University Popular Press, 1983.

Bruce, Janet. *The Kansas City Monarchs: Champions of Black Baseball*. Lawrence, Kansas: University Press of Kansas, 1985.

Burns, James MacGregor. "The Nation's Thrust to the Political Right in 1984." *Scholastic Update* 117 (December 14, 1984): 12.

Carnegie, Andrew. *The Empire of Business*. New York: Doubleday, Page & Co., 1902.

Caughey, John and Ernest May. *A History of the U.S.* Chicago: Rand McNally, 1964.

Clark, Kenneth E. "America Needs Heroes to Pull the Country Together." *U.S. News & World Report* 92 (June 7, 1982): 68.

Clemens, Samuel. *Mark Twain Speeches*. New York: Harper & Row Brothers, 1923.

Dickens, Charles. *A Tale of Two Cities*. New York: Grosset & Dunlap Publishers, 1948.

Dowdy, Andrew. *The Films of the Fifties: The American State of Mind*. New York: Morrow Books, 1973.

Egan, Jack. "Business: The Decade of the Deal." *U.S. News and World Report* 107 (December 25, 1989): 98

Elsinger, Chester E., ed., *The 1940's: Profile of a Nation in Crisis*. Documents on American Civilization Series. Garden City, New York: Anchor Books, 1969.

Etzioni, Amitai. "U.S. Needs a Moral and Social Recovery." *U.S. News and World Report* 96 (January 9, 1984): 59-60.

Etzioni, Amitai. "Once Again, an Era of Reconstruction Begins." *Scholastic Update* 117 (December 14, 1984): 8-9.

Fimrite, Ron. "A Star With Real Clout." *Sports Illustrated* 60 (May 7, 1984): 92-106.

Fitch, Janet. *"Field of Dreams*: Phil Alden Robinson on Deck." *American Film* 14 (May 1989): 62

Footlick, Jerrold K. "What Happened to the Family." *Newsweek* 114 (Winter/Spring 1990): 14-20.

Friedrich, Otto. "Freed from Greed." *Time* 135 (January 1, 1990): 76-78.

Giannetti, Louis. *Understanding Movies*, 4th ed. Englewood Cliffs, New Jersey: Prentice-Hall, Inc., 1987.

Gunther, John and Bernard Quint. *Days to Remember: America 1945-1955.* New York: Harper and Brothers, 1956.

Guttman, Allen. *From Ritual to Record.* New York: Columbia University Press, 1978.

Hamby, Alonzo L. *The Imperial Years: The U.S. Since 1939.* New York: Weybright and Talley, 1976.

Harpers. "Sports: How Dirty a Game?" 271 (September, 1985): 45-56.

Hart, Marie. *Sport in the Sociocultural Process,* 2nd ed., Dubuque, Iowa: Wm. C. Brown Company Publishers, 1976.

Head, Sydney and Christopher Sterling. *Broadcasting in America.* Boston: Houghton Mifflin Company, 1982.

Heath, Jim F. *Decade of Disillusionment.* Bloomington, Indiana: Indiana University Press, 1975.

Higham, Charles and Joel Greenberg. *Hollywood in the 40's.* New York: A.S. Barnes, 1968.

Hofstadter, Richard. *Anti-Intellectualism in American Life.* New York: Alfred A. Knopf, 1963.

Jackson, Kathy Merlock. *Images of Children in American Film.* Metuchen, New Jersey: Scarecrow Press, 1986.

Jowett, Garth. *Film: The Democratic Art.* Boston: Little, Brown, and Company, 1976.

Kariel, Henry. *The Decline of American Pluralism.* Stanford, California: Stanford University Press, 1965.

Keyser, Les and Barbara Keyser. *Hollywood and the Catholic Church.* Chicago: Loyola University Press, 1984.

Knight, Ann. "Baseball Like It Oughta Be." *American Film* 14 (May 1989): 76.

Kolko, Gabriel. *Main Currents in Modern American History.* New York: Harper & Row Publishers, 1976.

Kotsilibas-Davis, James and Myrna Loy. "Flashback: Being There." *American Film* 13:2 (November 1987): 22-25.

Kracauer, Siegfried. *From Caligari to Hitler.* Princeton, New Jersey: Princeton University Press, 1947.

Levine, Art. "Lifestyle: Having It All." *U.S. News and World Report* 107 (December 25, 1989 - January 1, 1990): 112-113.

Levine, Art. "Tom Wolfe: The Years of Living Prosperously." *U.S. News and World Report* 107 (December 25, 1989 - January 1, 1990): 117.

Lucas, John A. and Ronald A. Smith. *Saga of American Sport.* Philadelphia: Harper and Brothers Publishers, 1943.

McBee, Susanna. "Heroes Are Back." *U.S. News and World Report* 98 (April 22, 1985): 44-48.

MacDonald, Dwight. "The Candidates and I." *Commentary* 29 (April 1960): 287-294.

McGilligan, Pat. "The *American Film* Critics Poll: The 80s." *American Film* 15 (November 1989): 23-29.

MacKinnon, Kenneth. *Hollywood's Small Towns.* Metuchen, New Jersey: Scarecrow Press, 1984.

Magill's Survey of Cinema, Series II. Englewood Cliffs, New Jersey: Salem Press, 1986.

Malamud, Bernard. *The Natural.* New York: Farrar, Straus and Cudahy, 1952.

Manning, Robert, ed. *Viet Nam Experience: A Nation Divided*, Vol. II. Boston: Boston Publishing Company, 1984.

Marsden, Michael T., John G. Nachbar, and Sam L. Grogg, Jr., eds., *Movies as Artifacts*. Chicago: Nelson-Hall, Inc., 1982.

Miller, Annette. "The Great Housing Bust." *Newsweek* 114 (December 25, 1989): 54-55.

Miller, Douglas T., and Marion Nowalk. *The Fifties: The Way We Really Were*. New York: Doubleday, 1977.

Mitchell, Alice Miller, *Children and the Movies*. Chicago: University of Chicago Press, 1929.

Monroe, Cecil O. "The Rise of Baseball in Minnesota." *Minnesota History* 19 (June 1938).

Morris, Lloyd R. *Postscript to Yesterday: American Life and Thought 1896/ 1946*. New York: Harper and Row, 1947.

Mowry, George, ed., *The Twenties: Fords, Flappers and Fanatics*. Englewood Cliffs, New Jersey: Prentice-Hall, Inc., 1963.

Mowry, George. *The Urban Nation*. New York: Hill and Wang, 1965.

Nash, Jay Robert and Stanley Ralph Ross. *The Motion Picture Guide*. Chicago: Cinebooks, Inc., 1986.

Newman, Joseph, ed., *200 Years*. Washington, D.C.: Books By U.S. News & World Report, Inc., 1973.

New York Times. March 4, 1951. Sec. 5, p. 2.

New York Times. December 6, 1951. p. 34.

New York Times. "Transcript of Message by President on the State of the Union." January 26, 1984. Sec. B, p. 8.

The New York Times, Directory of the Film. New York: Arno Press, 1971.

Nugent, Frank S. *New York Times*. July 17, 1935. p. 22.

Nugent, Walter. *Structures of American Social History.* Bloomington, Indiana: Indiana University Press, 1981.

O'Connor, John E. and Martin A. Jackson, eds., *American History/American Film.* New York: Frederick Ungar Publishing Co., 1979.

O'Neill, William L. *Coming Apart.* Chicago: Quadrangle Books, 1971.

O'Neill, William L. *Everyone Was Brave.* Chicago: Quadrangle Books, 1969.

Peterson, Robert. *Only the Ball Was White.* Englewood Cliffs, New Jersey: Prentice-Hall, 1970.

Poynor, Alice. "Where Have All the Heroes Gone?" *Christianity Today* 28 (September 21, 1984): 82-83.

Quinn, Jane. "Growing Old Frugally." *Newsweek* 114 (Winter/Spring 1990): 102-105.

Rainie, Harrison. "Politics: Selling the Sizzle." *U.S. News and World Report* 107 (December 25, 1989 - January 1, 1990): 92-97.

Ray, Robert. *A Certain Tendency of the Hollywood Cinema, 1930-1980.* Princeton, New Jersey: Princeton University Press, 1985.

Reichler, Joe, ed. *Ronald Encyclopedia of Baseball.* New York: The Ronald Press Company, 1962.

Reichley, A. James. *Conservatives in an Age of Change.* Washington D.C.: The Brookings Institution, 1981.

Schlesinger, Arthur, Jr. "The Highbrows in Politics." *Partisan Review* 20 (March-April, 1953): 162-165.

Schwartz, Tony. *The Responsive Chord.* Garden City, New York: Anchor Press/Doubleday, 1973.

Sennewald, Andre. *New York Times.* February 18, 1932. p. 25.

Shlain, Bruce. "Whether It's Baseball or Acting, Kevin Costner's a Natural." *The Plain Dealer.* July 15, 1988. "Friday" Section, p. 26-27.

Short, K.R.M. *Feature Films as History*. Knoxville, Tennessee: The University of Tennessee Press, 1981.

Siegel, Frederick F. *Troubled Journey*. New York: Hill and Wang, 1984.

Sklar, Robert. *Movie-Made America*. New York: Random House, 1976.

Smelzer, Marshall. "The Babe on Balance." *The American Scholar* 44 (Spring 1975): 299-304.

Smith, Curt. *Voices of the Game*. South Bend, Indiana: Diamond Communications, Inc., 1987.

Sobol, Ken. *Babe Ruth and the American Dream*. New York: Ballantine Books, 1974.

Solomon, Stanley J. *Beyond Formula*. New York: Harcourt Brace Jovanovich, Inc., 1976.

Somers, Dale A. "The Leisure Revolution: Recreation In the American City, 1820-1920." *Journal of Popular Culture* 5 (Summer 1971): 125-147.

Spock, Benjamin. "It's All Up to Us." *Newsweek* 114 (Winter/Spring 1990): 106-107.

Steinberg, Cobbett S. *Film Facts*. New York: Facts on File, Inc., 1980.

Sugar, Bert Randolph. *Baseball's 50 Greatest Games*. New York: Exeter Books, 1986.

Thomson, David. "Michael Douglas: Business as Usual." *Film Comment* 26 (January-February 1990): 16-21.

Time 40 (July 6, 1942): 81.

Time 63 (April 26, 1954): 104.

Turner, Frederick Jackson. "The Significance of the Frontier in American History," rpt. *The Frontier in American History*. New York: Holt, Rinehart, and Winston, 1962.

U.S.A. Today. "Baseball's on Screen Hits and Errors." April 6, 1987. Sec. E., 11.

U.S. News 32 (May 16, 1952): 16.

U.S. News & World Report 84 (March 27, 1978): 38-43.

Umphlett, Wiley Lee, ed. *American Sport Culture*. Cranbury, New Jersey: Bucknell University Press, 1985.

Variety 177 (January 4, 1950): 59.

Variety 229 (January 9, 1963): 13.

Variety 273 (January 9, 1974): 19 and 60.

Variety 313 (January 9, 1984): 80.

Variety 317 (January 16, 1985): 16.

Variety 318 (February 13, 1985): 34.

Vinson, James, ed., *International Dictionary of Films and Filmmakers:* volume III. Chicago: St. James Press, 1986.

Wood, Michael. *America in the Movies*. New York: Basic Books, 1975.

Zucker, Harvey Marc and Lawrence J. Babich. *Sports Films: A Complete Reference*. Jefferson, North Carolina: McFarland and Company, Inc., 1987.

Appendix: List of Baseball Films (1929-1989)

Movie		Year	Studio
	Fast Company	1929	Paramount Famous Lasky
	They Learned About Women	1930	MGM
	Hot Curves	1930	Tiffany Productions
*	Fireman, Save My Child	1932	Warner Bros.
*	Elmer the Great	1933	Warner Bros.
	Swell-Head	1935	Columbia
*	Alibi Ike	1935	Warner Bros.
	It Happened in Flatbush	1942	20th Century-Fox
	Moonlight in Havana	1942	Universal
#	Pride of the Yankees	1942	RKO Radio Pictures
*	Ladies' Day	1943	RKO Radio Pictures
*	Babe Ruth Story	1948	Monogram Pictures
#	It Happens Every Spring	1949	20th Century-Fox
#	The Stratton Story	1949	MGM
#	Take Me Out to the Ball Game	1949	MGM
	Kid from Cleveland	1949	Republic
*	Jackie Robinson Story	1950	Eagle Lion Films
	Kill the Umpire	1950	Columbia
#	Rhubarb	1951	Paramount
#	Angels in the Outfield	1951	MGM
*	Pride of St. Louis	1952	20th Century-Fox
#	Winning Team	1952	Warner Bros.
#	Kid from Left Field	1953	20th Century-Fox
#	Big Leaguer	1953	MGM
	Roogie's Bump	1954	Republic
	Great American Pastime	1956	MGM
#	Fear Strikes Out	1957	Paramount

167

#	Damn Yankees	1958	Warner Bros.
*	Safe at Home	1962	Columbia
#	Bang the Drum Slowly	1973	Paramount
#	Bad News Bears	1976	Paramount
#	Bingo Long Traveling All-Stars and Motor Kings	1976	Universal
*	Bad News Bears in Breaking Training	1977	Paramount
*	Here Come the Tigers	1978	American-International
*	Bad News Bears Go to Japan	1978	Paramount
*	Blue Skies Again	1983	Warner Bros.
*	Natural	1984	Tri-Star Pictures
*	Bull Durham	1988	Orion
*	Eight Men Out	1988	Orion
*	Major League	1989	Paramount
*	Field of Dreams	1989	Universal

* Indicates that the film version was viewed.
\# Indicates that a video copy was viewed.

Index